Horatius Bonar

The Bible Hymn-book

Horatius Bonar

The Bible Hymn-book

ISBN/EAN: 9783744779463

Printed in Europe, USA, Canada, Australia, Japan

Cover: Foto ©Lupo / pixelio.de

More available books at **www.hansebooks.com**

THE

BIBLE HYMN-BOOK.

EDITED BY THE

REV. HORATIUS BONAR.

"Let the children of Zion be joyful in their King."—Ps. cxlix. 2.

NEW YORK:
ROBERT CARTER AND BROTHERS,
530 BROADWAY.
1860.

PREFACE.

This Hymn-Book is designed both for general use and for Sabbath Schools. In compiling it, both objects have been carefully kept in view, so that "young men and maidens, old men and children," may use it in praising the name of the Lord.

The Hymns have been drawn together from a great variety of sources, both ancient and modern, and no small pains have been taken to render the selection both choice and complete. While all the well-known favourites have been retained, a large number have been added hitherto but little known.

"Let the word of Christ dwell in you richly, in all wisdom, teaching and admonishing one another in psalms, and hymns, and spiritual songs; singing with grace in your hearts to the Lord."

INDEX.

	HYMN		HYMN
Act but the infant's	83	Children of light	156
Ah, I shall soon	91	Christ, the Lord	171
Ah! my dear Lord	140	Christ, whose glory	50
All glory to the	172	Clear spring of life	55
All hail the power	291	Cling to the crucified	270
All that we are	215	Come, my fond	153
All that I was	220	Come to the ark	144
And is the gospel	148	Come, wandering	137
Angels holy	90	Come, thou fount	57
A pilgrim through	273	Come, ye sinners	149
Arise my tend'rest	79	Come, ye souls	150
Arise ye saints	188	Commit thou all	234
Art thou weak	12	Cross, reproach	232
Art thou a child	45	Day of judgment	139
As a little weaned	81	Dear Lord, amid	192
Asleep in Jesus	218	Dear Lord! though	199
Awake, my soul	131	Does the Gospel	151
Awake, my heart	163	Fair are the feet	119
Awake, and sing	286	Farewell, ye fleeting	259
Behold the Lamb	285	Far from home	287
Behold the man	191	Far from these	43
Beloved, "it is well"	32	Far from the world	133
Beloved Saviour	107	Flow fast, my tears	167
Be steady, be steady	117	For ever here	180
Blessed be God	225	For ever to behold	271
Bliss beyond	68	For ever with	242
Blow ye the trumpet	20	For thee we long	65
Bread of the world	157	Forward let the	13
Bride of the Lamb	209	From Greenland's	127
Brother—would'st	187	Give to the winds	235
Call Jehovah	70	Gloomy and dark	210
Cheer up, my soul	252	Glorious things	112

INDEX.

	HYMN		HYMN
Sweet Jesus! when	101	To Calvary, Lord	263
Sweet the moment	49	To thee my heart	75
Sweet was	26	To watch	103
Sweet was the hour	174	Walk in the light	268
Teach me yet more	42	Watchman! tell us	111
That I am thine	223	We go with	60
That clime is not	297	Welcome, sweet day	67
The ancient days	142	We seek a rest	246
The atoning work	248	We sing to God	130
The blood of Christ	258	We sing the praise	267
The Church	301	What a rapturous	299
The cross, the cross	236	What earthly thing	124
The God of Abraham	5	What grace, O Lord	74
The happy morn	170	What is this life	36
"The Lord is risen"	169	What must it be	229
The morning	118	What, tho' time	11
The Son of God	222	What various	6
There in peace	241	When friend	29
There is a fountain	145	When quiet	24
There is a path	147	When the spark	47
There is a sacred	168	When the vale	63
There is a morning	280	When a careless	154
There is a land	296	When this passing	201
There is a stream	298	When heaves	205
There was gladness	92	When I survey	225
Think not that e'er	95	While in sweet	99
This is not my place	260	While to Bethlehem	185
Thou, great	284	While we remember	217
Tho' twice ten	178	Who but a Christian	158
Tho' the heart	261	Who hath our report	121
Thousands of	17	Why fear the path	44
Thou who didst	78	Why did the paschal	212
Thy ways, O Lord	38	With Heaven	253
Time's sun is fast	295	With sweet	237
'Tis come, the glad	146	Ye blest domestics	288
"'Tis finished,"	193	Ye holy angels bright	89
'Tis He! the mighty	161	Yes, the Christian's	243
'Tis my happiness	200	Ye virgin souls	155
'Tis past, the dark	269		

THE BIBLE HYMN-BOOK.

I.

"In the beginning God created the heavens and the earth."—Gen. i. 1.

1 In the beginning was THE WORD;
    The Word was God.
  In the beginning was the Word;
    And His abode
    From everlasting was with God.
        His name
        I AM,—
    Jehovah, God, the Lord,
    Ever to be adored:
    The eternal Son,—
    The ever-blessed One.
  From all, to all eternity,
  The brightness of the eternal Father's glory He.

2 Creator of the heaven and earth,
    Their Lord and King.

Creator of the heaven and earth,
    The angels sing!
    To him all praise and glory bring;
      His power
      Adore,
    From which all things had birth,
    By which they still stand forth
  In beauty glad,
    With heav'nly radiance clad.
Praise, praise His ever-flowing love,
That brightens all below and gladdens all above.

3 "Let there be light,"—'twas He that spoke,—
    "And there was light."
  "Let there be light,"—'twas He that spoke,—
    And the long night
    At His divine command took flight.
      The ray
      Of day
    O'er the deep darkness broke;
    The sleeping world awoke:
  Earth, sea and sky
  Burst forth in praises high
To Him who made the light to be:—   [He!
He is the Light of light, and there is none but

II.

ANOTHER OF THE SAME.

1 OUR God is good, and he is great,
Around His throne the angels wait:
He made the sun with beams so bright,
He made the moon which shines by night,—
The glittering skies that look so fair,
With every star that sparkles there.

2 The mountains and the rocks he made,
And all the hills in order laid:
He poured the water in the seas;
He made the grass, the herbs the trees,—
The valleys and the fields so fair,
And every flower that blossoms there.

3 The lion and the tiger bold,
The sheep and cattle of the fold;
The little birds that sweetly sing,
The insect with its beauteous wing;
The fishes—all we see that's fair
Or good,—He made, and placed them there.

III.

"And God saw everything that He had made, and behold it was very good."—Gen. i. 31.

1 How goodly is the earth!
　　Look round about and see
　The green and fruitful field,
　　The mighty branchèd tree,
　The little flowers out-spread
　　In such variety.
　Behold the lovely things
　That float on airy wings;
　Behold the radiant isles
　With which old ocean smiles;
　The clouds that lie at rest
　Upon the noon-day's breast:
　　Behold all these, and know
　　　How goodly is the earth!

2 How goodly is the earth!
　　Its mountain-tops behold;
　Its rivers broad and strong,
　　Its forests dark and old,
　Its wealth of flocks and herds,
　　Its precious stones and gold.

Behold the seasons run
Obedient to the sun ;
The gracious showers descend,—
Life springing without end,—
By day the glorious light,
The starry pomp by night:
 Behold all these, and know
 How goodly is the earth!

3 How goodly is the earth!
Yet, if this earth be made
So goodly, wherein all
 That is, shall droop and fade,
Wherein the glorious light
 Hath still its darkening shade ;
Where trouble dims the eye,
Where sin hath mastery ;
How much more bright and fair
Will be that region where
The Saints of God shall rest
With Jesus, and be blest;
 Where pain is not, nor death,—
 The Paradise of God!

IV.

"Enoch walked with God."—Gen. v. 24.

1 Oh! for a closer walk with God,
    A calm and heav'nly frame;
  A light to shine upon the road
    That leads me to the Lamb!

2 Where is the blessedness I knew,
    When first I saw the Lord ?
  Where is the soul-refreshing view
    Of Jesus and His word ?

3 What peaceful hours I once enjoy'd,
    How sweet their mem'ry still !
  But they have left an aching void,
    The world can never fill.

4 Return, O holy Dove, return !
    Sweet messenger of rest;
  I hate the sins that made thee mourn,
    And drove thee from my breast.

5 The dearest idol I have known,
    Whate'er that idol be,

Help me to tear it from thy throne,
And worship only thee.

6 So shall my walk be close with God,
Calm and serene my frame;
So purer light shall mark the road
That leads me to the Lamb.

V.

" And when Abram was ninety years old and nine, the Lord appeared to Abram, and said unto him, I am the Almighty God."—Gen. xxvii. 1.

1 THE God of Abraham praise,
Who reigns enthroned above;
Ancient of everlasting days,
And God of love;
Jehovah, Great I Am!
By earth and heaven confessed;
I bow and bless the sacred name,
For ever bless'd.

2 The God of Abraham praise,
  At whose supreme command
From earth I rise—and seek the joys
    At his right hand;
  I all on earth forsake,
  Its wisdom, fame and power,
And him my only portion make,
    My shield and tower.

3 The God of Abraham praise,
  Whose all-sufficient grace
Shall guide me all my happy days,
    In all his ways:
  He calls a worm his friend!
  He calls Himself my God!
And He shall save me to the end,
    Through Jesus' blood.

4 He by Himself hath sworn,
  I on His oath depend,
I shall, on eagles' wings up-borne,
    To heaven ascend:
  I shall behold His face,
  I shall His power adore,
And sing the wonders of His grace
    For evermore.

5 Though nature's strength decay,
And earth and hell withstand,
To Canaan's bounds I urge my way,
At His command :
The watery deep I pass,
With Jesus in my view ;
And through the howling wilderness,
My way pursue.

6 The goodly land I see,
With peace and plenty bless'd ;
A land of sacred liberty,
And endless rest :
There milk and honey flow,
And oil and wine abound ;
And trees of life for ever grow,
With mercy crown'd.

7 There dwells the Lord our King,
The Lord our Righteousness,
Triumphant o'er the world and sin,
The Prince of Peace :
On Sion's sacred height
His kingdom still maintains ;
And glorious, with his saints in light
For ever reigns.

8 He keeps His own secure,
   He guards them by His side,
Arrays in garments white and pure,
   His spotless bride;
With streams of sacred bliss,
   With groves of living joys,
With all the fruits of paradise,
   He still supplies.

9 Before the Three in One,
   They all exulting stand;
And tell the wonders He hath done,
   Through all their land.
The listening spheres attend,
   And swell the growing fame,
And sing in songs which never end,
   The wondrous Name.

10 The God who reigns on high,
   The great arch-angels sing,
And " Holy, Holy, Holy," cry,
   " Almighty King!
Who was, and is the same,
   And evermore shall be;
Jehovah—Father—Great I Am!
   We worship thee."

11   Before the Saviour's face
    The ransomed nations bow;
    O erwhelmed at his Almighty grace,
        For ever new :
    He shows his prints of love,
    They kindle to a flame,
    And sound, through all the world above,
        The slaughter'd Lamb.

12   The whole triumphant host
    Give thanks to God on high;
    Hail, Father, Son and Holy Ghost,
        They ever cry.
    Hail, Abraham's God and mine.
    I join the heavenly lays;
    All might and majesty are thine,
        And endless praise.

VI.

"Escape for thy life; look not behind thee, neither stay thou in all the plain."—Gen. xix. 17.

1 HASTEN, O sinner, to be wise,
    And stay not for the morrow's sun;

The longer Wisdom you despise,
　　The harder is she to be won.

2 O hasten, mercy to implore,
　　And stay not for the morrow's sun;
　For fear thy season should be o'er
　　Before this evening's stage be run.

3 O hasten, sinner, to return,
　　And stay not for the morrow's sun,
　For fear thy lamp should fail to burn
　　Before thy needful work is done.

4 O hasten, sinner, to be blest,
　　And stay not for the morrow's sun,
　For fear the curse should thee arrest
　　Before the morrow is begun.

5 O Lord do thou the sinner turn!
　　Now rouse him from his senseless state!
　O let him not thy counsel spurn,
　　Nor rue his fatal choice too late!

VII.

"Escape to the mountain, lest thou be consumed."
—Gen. xix. 17.

1 HASTE, traveller, haste! the night comes on,
And many a shining hour is gone;
The storm is gathering in the west,
And thou art far from home and rest;
  Haste, traveller, haste!

2 O, far from home thy footsteps stray;
Christ is the life, and Christ the way,
And Christ the light. Yon setting sun
Sinks ere the morn is scarce begun:
  Haste, traveller, haste!

3 The rising tempest sweeps the sky,
The rains descend, the winds are high;
The waters swell, and death and fear
Beset thy path—no refuge near:
  Haste, traveller, haste!

4 O yes, a shelter you may gain,—
A covert from the wind and rain,—

A hiding place, a rest, a home,—
A refuge from the wrath to come:
        Haste, traveller, haste!

5 Then linger not in all the plain,
Flee for thy life, the mountain gain;
Look not behind, make no delay,
O, speed thee, speed thee on thy way:
        Haste, traveller, haste!

6 Poor, lost, benighted soul, art thou
Willing to find salvation now?—
There yet is hope,—hear mercy's call,—
Truth, life, light, way, in Christ is all!
        Haste to HIM, haste!

VIII.

"I am with thee, and will keep thee in all places whether thou goest."—Gen. xxviii. 15.

1 On mountains and in valleys,.
    Where'er we go is God;
The cottage and the palace
    Alike are His abode.

2 In sinking and in soaring,
  Thought finds him ever near,—
Where angels are adoring,
  Where fiends believe and fear.

3 With watchful eye abiding
  Upon us with delight;
Our souls, in Him confiding,
  He keeps both day and night.

4 Above me, and beside me,
  My God is ever near,—
To watch, protect and guide me,
  Whatever ills appear.

5 Tho' other friends may fail me
  In sorrow's dark abode,—
Tho' death itself assail me,
  I'm ever safe with God.

IX.

"I will not let thee go except thou bless me."—
Gen. xxxii. 26.

1 Nay, I cannot let thee go,
Till a blessing thou bestow;
Do not turn away thy face
Mine's an urgent, pressing case.

2 Dost thou ask me who I am?
Ah, my Lord, thou know'st my name!
Yet the question gives a plea,
To support my suit with thee.

3 Thou didst once a wretch behold,
In rebellion blindly bold,
Scorn thy grace. thy pow'r defy,
That poor rebel, Lord, was I.

4 Once a sinner near despair
Sought thy mercy-seat by pray'r;
Mercy heard and set him free,
Lord, that mercy came to me.

5 Many years have passed since then,
Many changes I have seen,
Yet have been upheld till now;
Who could hold me up but thou?

6 Thou hast help'd in every need,
This emboldens me to plead;
After so much mercy past,
Canst thou let me sink at last?

7 No—I must maintain my hold,
'Tis thy goodness makes me bold;
I can no denial take,
When I plead for Jesus' sake.

X.

ANOTHER OF THE SAME.

1 LIKE Jacob here I stand,
  And wrestle with the Lord;
With weary heart and hand,
  Waiting some gracious word.
Waiting some gracious word
  To soothe my heavy woe:—
Except thou bless me, Lord,
  I will not let thee go.

2 The day is breaking fast,
 All night I have been here,
To cure my aching breast,
 When shall my Lord appear?
When shall my Lord appear,
 And comfort to me flow?
Except thou bless me, Lord,
 I will not let thee go.

XI.

'I have waited for thy salvation, O Lord."—Gen. xlix. 18.

1 What tho' time on earth were over,
 Not on time our hopes depend;
Lo, beyond it, we discover
 Life that never knows an end.
'Mid the woes that life attend,
 Still for rest we turn to thee:
God, a father and a friend,
 Changeless, in his Son we see.

2 Father still in all our need,
 Father still in weal or woe;

Father even of the dead,
　When into the grave we go.
Change may toss us to and fro,
　Changeless He in whom we trust:
Ev'n our dust his care shall know,
　When our bodies turn to dust.

3 Then let days and years be fleeting,
　Swiftly pass our joys and woes;
'Mid the changes we are meeting,
　God, our God, no changes knows.
Our's be then a life that shows
　That conducted by his hand,
We shall enter at its close
　Our beloved father-land.

XII.

"I am."—Exod. iii. 14.

Art thou weak, afflicted soul?
I am strong to make thee whole.
Art thou sick and hast no cure?
I am thy physician sure.
Art thou fainting on thy road?
I am near to bear thy load.

Art thou hungry, thirsty, poor?
I am rich to bless thy store.
Art thou much with grief opprest?
I am come to give thee rest.
Art thou weary of thy sin?
I am peace to thee within.
I am ready at thy side,
At thy right and left to guide.
I am life, and love, and peace,—
I am joy which ne'er shall cease.

XIII.

"Speak unto the children of Israel, that they go forward."—Exod. xiv. 15.

1 "Forward let the people go,"
   Israel's God will have it so:
   Though the path be through the sea,
   Israel what is that to thee?
He who bids thee pass the waters
Will be with his sons and daughters.

2 Deep and wide the sea appears:
   Israel wonders—Israel fears—

Yet the word is " Forward" still :
Israel ! 'tis the Master's will ;
Though no way thou can'st discover,
Not one plank to float thee over.

3 Israel, art thou sorely tried ?
Art thou press'd on every side ?
Does it seem as if no power
Could relieve thee in this hour ?
Wherefore art thou thus disheartened,
Is the arm that saves thee shortened ?

4 Stand thou still this day, and see
Wonders wrought, and wrought for thee :
Safe thyself on yonder shore,
Thou shalt see thy foes no more.
Thine to see the Saviour's glory,
Thine to tell the wond'rous story.

5 Yes, thy God shall yet be known,
Far and wide, as God alone :
At his feet shall idols fall,
For thy God is Lord of all.
His is strength, and his salvation,—
He shall reign o'er ev'ry nation.

XIV.

"My father's God, I will exalt Him."—Exod. xv. 2.

1 O God, our help in ages past,
    Our hope for years to come,
Our shelter from the stormy blast,
    And our eternal home.

2 Under the shadow of thy throne,
    Thy saints have dwelt secure,
Sufficient is thine arm alone,
    And our defence is sure.

3 Thro' every scene of life and death
    Thy promise is our trust,
And this shall be our children's song
    When we are cold in dust.

4 O God, our help in ages past,
    Our hope for years to come;
Be thou our guard while life shall last,
    And our eternal home.

XV.

"I am the Lord that healeth thee."—Exod. xv. 26

1 HEAL us, Emmanuel, here we are,
  Waiting to feel thy touch :
  Deep-wounded souls to thee repair,
  And, Saviour, we are such.

2 Our faith is feeble, we confess,
  We faintly trust thy word ;
  But wilt thou pity us the less ?
  Be that far from thee, Lord !

3 Remember him who once applied
  With trembling for relief ;
  " Lord, I believe," with tears he cried,
  " O help my unbelief !"

4 She too, who touch'd thee in the press,
  And healing virtue stole,
  Was answer'd, " Daughter, go in peace,
  Thy faith hath made thee whole."

5 Conceal'd amid the gath'ring throng,
   She would have shunn'd thy view;
And if her faith was firm and strong,
   Had strong misgivings too.

6 Like her, with hopes and fears we come,
   To touch thee if we may;
Oh! send us not despairing home,
   Send none unheal'd away.

XVI.

"It came to pass when Moses held up his hand that Israel prevailed."—Exod. xvii. 11.

1 What various hind'rances we meet
  In coming to a mercy seat?
  Yet who that knows the worth of pray'r,
  But wishes to be often there?

2 Pray'r makes the darken'd cloud withdraw,
  Pray'r climbs the ladder Jacob saw,
  Gives exercise to faith and love,
  Brings ev'ry blessing from above.

3 Restraining pray'r, we cease to fight;
  Pray'r makes the Christian's armour bright;

And Satan trembles when he sees
The weakest saint upon his knees.

4 While Moses stood with arms spread wide,
Success was found on Israel's side ;
But when through weariness they fail'd,
That moment Amalek prevailed.

5 Have you no words? Ah! think again,
Words flow apace when you complain,
And fill your fellow-creature's ear
With the sad tale of all your care.

6 Were half the breath thus vainly spent,
To Heav'n in supplication sent,
Your cheerful song would oft'ner be,
" Hear what the Lord has done for me."

XVII.

"I beseech thee show me thy glory."—Exod.
xxxiii. 18.

1 Thousands of thousands stand around
    Thy throne, O God most high!
Ten thousand times ten thousand sound
    Thy praise—but who am I?

2 Thy brightness unto them appears,
   Whilst I thy footsteps trace:
A sound of God comes to my ears,
   But they behold thy face.

3 How great a being, Lord, is thine,
   Which doth all beings keep!
Thy knowledge is the only line
   To sound so vast a deep.

4 How good art Thou, whose goodness is
   Our parent, nurse, and guide:
Whose streams do water Paradise,
   And all this earth beside.

5 Thine upper and thy nether springs
   Make both thy worlds to thrive;
Under thy warm and sheltering wings,
   Thou keep'st two broods alive.

6 Thy arm of might, most mighty King,
   Both rocks and hearts doth break:
My God, thou canst do every thing,
   But what should show thee weak.

7 How awful is thy searching eye,
   Witness to all that's true!
   Dark hell, and deep hypocrisy
   Lie plain before its view.

8 Most pure and holy are thine eyes,
   Most holy is thy name;
   Thy saints, and laws, and penalties,
   Thy holiness proclaim.

9 Mercy, that shining attribute,
   The sinner's hope and plea;
   Huge hosts of sins in their pursuit
   Are drown'd in that Red Sea.

10 Thy wisdom, which both makes and mends,
   We ever must admire:
   Creation all our wit transcends;
   Redemption rises higher.

11 Great is thy truth, and shall prevail
   To unbelievers' shame;
   Thy truth and years do never fail,
   Thou ever art the same.

12 Unbelief is a raging wave
    Dashing against a rock;
If God doth not his Israel save,
    Then let the Egyptians mock.

13 Thy bright back-parts, O God of grace,
    I humbly here adore;
Show me thy glory and thy face,
    That I may praise thee more.

XVIII.

"He put the breastplate upon him, also he put in the breastplate the Urim and the Thummim."—Lev. viii. 8.

1 SEE Aaron, God's anointed priest,
    Within the veil appear,
In robes of mystic meaning drest,
    Presenting Israel's prayer.

2 The plate of gold which crowns his brow,
    His holiness describes;
His breast displays in shining rows
    The names of all the tribes.

3 With the atoning blood he stands
   Before the mercy seat ;
And clouds of incense from his hands
   Arise with odour sweet.

4 Urim and Thummim near his heart,
   In rich engravings worn,
The sacred light of truth impart,
   To teach and to adorn.

5 Through him the eye of faith descries
   A greater priest than he ;
Thus Jesus pleads above the skies,
   For you, my friends, and me.

6 He bears the names of all his saints
   Deep on his heart engrav'd ;
Attentive to the state and wants
   Of all his love has sav'd.

7 In him a holiness complete,
   Light and perfections shine ;
And wisdom, grace, and glory meet ;
   A Saviour all divine.

8 The blood, which as a priest he bears
    For sinners, is his own;
The incense of his pray'rs and tears
    Perfumes the holy throne.

9 In him my weary soul has rest,
    Though I am weak and vile;
I read my name upon his breast,
    And see the Father's smile.

XIX.

"Aaron went unto the altar, and slew the calf of the sin-offering which was for himself."—Lev. ix. 8.

1 Jesus, in thee our eyes behold
    A thousand glories more
Than the rich gems and polish'd gold,
    The sons of Aaron wore.

2 They first their own sin-offering brought
    To purge themselves from sin;
Thy life was pure without a spot,
    And all thy nature clean.

3 Fresh blood, as constant as the day,
   Was on their altars spilt;
But thy one offering took away
   For ever all our guilt.

4 Thou, great Melchizedec! shalt reign
   In peace on Zion's hill,
(Thyself the Lamb that once was slain,)
   And bear thy priesthood still.

5 Till then, for us to intercede
   Before the Father's face,
Be this thy work, and ours to plead
   Thy merits, and His grace.

XX.

"In the day of atonement shall ye make the trumpet sound."—Lev. xxv. 9.

1 Blow ye the trumpet, blow!
   The gladly solemn sound!
Let all the nations know,
   To earth's remotest bound,
      The year of Jubilee is come,
      Return ye ransom'd sinners home.

2 Exalt the Lamb of God,
 The sin-atoning Lamb;
Redemption by his blood
 Thro' all the lands proclaim.
  The year, &c.

3 Ye who have sold for nought
 The heritage above,
Shall have it back unbought,
 The gift of Jesus' love.
  The year, &c.

4 Ye slaves of sin and hell,
 Your liberty receive,
And safe in Jesus dwell,
 And bless'd in Jesus live.
  The year, &c.

5 The gospel trumpet hear,
 The news of pard'ning grace;
Ye happy souls draw near,
 Behold your Saviour's face.
  The year, &c.

6 Jesus our great high-priest,
 Has full atonement made;

Ye weary spirits rest,
Ye mournful souls be glad.
The year, &c.

XXI.

"It shall be said of Jacob and of Israel, what hath God wrought."—Num. xxiii. 23.

1 God moves in a mysterious way
 His wonders to perform;
 He plants his footsteps in the sea,
 And rides upon the storm.

2 Deep in unfathomable mines
 Of never-failing skill,
 He treasures up his bright designs,
 And works his sov'reign will.

3 Ye fearful saints, fresh courage take,
 The clouds ye so much dread
 Are big with mercy, and shall break
 In blessings on your head.

4 Judge not the Lord by feeble sense,
 But trust him for his grace;
 Behind a frowning providence
 He hides a smiling face.

5 His purposes will ripen fast,
   Unfolding every hour;
The bud may have a bitter taste,
   But sweet will be the flow'r.

6 Blind unbelief is sure to err,
   And scan his work in vain:
God is his own interpreter,
   And he will make it plain.

XXII.

"There shall come a star out of Jacob, and a sceptre out of Israel."—Num. xxiv. 17.

1 O Earth, rejoice! from Salem see
   The chosen heralds bear
Glad tidings to the distant isles,
   That Salem's King is there.

2 Lo, Jacob's star, in vision seen
   By Balaam's wond'ring eye!
It bursts upon the nations now,
   The day-spring from on high.

3 A crown, but not a crown of thorn,
   Surrounds the Victor's brow ;
   That hand that once was pierced for sin,
   It wields the sceptre now,

4 But brighter honours far than those
   Of David's royal son,
   As Head of His anointed bride,
   The Lord of Life hath won.

5 Though grace may shine in all his ways,
   With Israel's chosen race ;
   'Tis in his church alone we see,
   The full display of grace.

6 'Twas grace divine that made him love,
   And choose her for His own :
   Grace raised her from her low estate,
   And placed her on the throne.

XXIII.

"Thou shalt love the Lord thy God with all thine heart."—Deut. vi. 5.

1 O lov'd, but not enough ; tho' dearer far
Than self, and its most lov'd enjoyments are !
None duly loves thee, but who nobly free
From sensual objects, finds his all in thee.

2 Glorious, Almighty, first, and without end !
When wilt thou melt the mountains, and descend ?
When wilt thou shoot abroad thy conquering rays,
And teach these atoms thou hast made thy praise ?

XXIV.

"Thou shalt talk of them when thou sittest in thine house, and when thou walkest by the way."—Deut. vi. 7.

1 When quiet in my house I sit,
    Thy book be my companion still,
My joy thy sayings to repeat,—
    Talk o'er the records of thy will,
And search the oracles divine,
Till every heartfelt word be mine.

2 O may the gracious words divine,
    Subject of all my converse be;
  So will the Lord his follower join,
    And walk and talk himself with me;
  So shall my heart his presence prove,
  And burn with everlasting love.

3 Oft as I lay me down to rest,
    O, may the reconciling word
  Sweetly compose my weary breast!
    While on the bosom of my Lord
  I sink in blissful dreams away,—
  And visions of eternal day.

4 Rising to sing my Saviour's praise,
    Thee may I publish all day long;
  And let thy precious word of grace
    Flow from my heart and fill my tongue!
  Fill all my life with purest love,
  And join me to the church above.

XXV.

"Happy art thou, O Israel: who is like unto thee, O people saved by the Lord."—Deut. xxxiii. 29.

1 O Israel, who is like to thee?
   A people sav'd, and call'd to be
      Peculiar to the Lord?
   Thy shield! he guards thee from the foe;
   Thy sword! he fights thy battles too,
      Himself thy great reward.

2 Thy toils have almost reach'd a close,
   Thou soon art destined to repose
      Within the promised land:
   Its rising hills ev'n now are seen
   Enrich'd with everlasting green,
      Where thou so soon shalt stand.

3 Sweet hope! it makes the coward brave,
   It makes a freeman of the slave,
      And bids the sluggard rise;
   It lifts a worm of earth on high,
   It gives him wings, and bids him fly
      To everlasting joys.

XXVI.

"So Moses, the servant of the Lord died there, in the land of Moab."—Deut. xxxiv. 5.

1 Sweet was the journey to the sky
　　The holy prophet tried ;
"Climb up the mount," said God, "and die ;"
　　The prophet climb'd and died.

2 Softly, with fainting head, he lay
　　Upon his Maker's breast ;
His Maker soothed his soul away,
　　And laid his flesh to rest.

3 In God's own arms he left the breath
　　That God's own Spirit gave ;
His was the noblest road to death,
　　And his the sweetest grave.

XXVII.

"Behold this day I am going the way of all the earth."—Josh. xxiii. 14.

1 My span of life will soon be done,
　　The passing moments say ;

As lengthening shadows o'er the plain
   Proclaim the close of day.

2 Soon will the toilsome strife be o'er
   Of weariness and care;
  And life's dull vanities no more
   This anxious heart ensnare.

3 Courage, my soul! thy bitter cross,
   In every trial here,
  Shall bear thee to thy heaven above,
   But shall not enter there.

4 Courage, my soul! on God rely,
   Deliverance soon shall come;
  A thousand ways thy Saviour has
   To bring his people home.

XXVIII.

"It is the Lord, let Him do what seemeth Him good."—1 Sam. iii. 18.

1 It is the Lord—enthroned in light,
   Whose claims are all divine;
  Who has an undisputed right
   To govern me and mine.

2 It is the Lord—should I distrust
    Or contradict his will,
  Who cannot do but what is just,
    And must be righteous still?

3 It is the Lord—who gives me all,—
    My wealth, my friends, my ease;
  And of His bounties may recall
    Whatever part He please.

4 It is the Lord—who can sustain
    Beneath the heaviest load:
  From whom assistance I obtain,
    To tread the thorny road.

5 It is the Lord—whose matchless skill
    Can from afflictions raise
  Blessings, eternity to fill
    With ever-growing praise.

6 It is the Lord—my covenant God,
    Thrice blessed be his name,
  Whose gracious promise, sealed with blood,
    Must ever be the same.

XXIX.

"And Jonathan said to David, Go in peace, forasmuch as we have sworn both of us in the name of the Lord, saying, the Lord be between me and thee."—1 Sam. xx. 42.

1 When friend from friend is parting,
    And in each speaking eye
The silent tear is starting,
    To tell what words deny,—
How could we bear the heavy load
    Of such heart-agony,
Could we not cast it all, our God,
    Our gracious God, on thee:
And feel that thou kind watch wilt keep
    When we are far away,—
That thou wilt soothe us when we weep,
    And hear us when we pray.

2 Yet oft these hearts will whisper—
    That better 'twould betide,
If we were near the friends we love,
    And watching by their side;
But sure thou'lt love them dearer, Lord,
    For trusting thee alone,

And sure thou wilt draw nearer, Lord,
  The farther we are gone:
Then why be sad, since thou wilt keep
  Watch o'er them night and day?
Since thou wilt soothe them when they weep,
  And hear us when we pray.

3 O for that bright and happy land,
  Where, far amid the blest,
The wicked cease from troubling, and
  The weary are at rest!
Where friends are never parted,
  Once met around thy throne:
And none are broken-hearted,
  Since all with thee are one!
Yet, Oh, till then, watch o'er us keep,
  While far from thee away,
And soothe us, Lord, oft as we weep,
  And hear us when we pray.

XXX.

"Is this thy kindness to thy friend?"—2 Sam.
  xvi. 17.

1 Poor, weak, and worthless, though I am,
  I have a rich, Almighty friend;

Jesus, the Saviour, is his name,
   He freely loves, and without end.

2 He ransom'd me from hell with blood,
   And by his power, my foes controll'd;
He found me wand'ring far from God,
   And brought me to his chosen fold.

3 He cheers my heart, my wants supplies,
   And says that I shall shortly be
Enthron'd with him above the skies:
   Oh! what a friend is Christ to me!

4 But ah! my inmost spirit mourns,
   And well my eyes with tears may swim,
To think of my perverse returns;
   I've been a faithless friend to him.

5 Before the world that hates his cause,
   My treach'rous heart has throbb'd with shame;
Loath to forego the world's applause,
   I hardly dare avow his name.

6 Sure were I not most vile and base,
   I could not thus my friend requite!
And were not he the God of grace,
   He'd frown and spurn me from his sight.

XXXI.

"He shall be as the light of the morning, when the sun riseth."—2 Sam. xxiii. 4.

1 Light for the dreary vales
    Of ice-bound Labrador!
  Where the frost-king breathes on the slippery sails,
    And the mariner wakes no more;
  Lift high the lamp that never fails,
    To that dark and sterile shore.

2 Light for the forest child!
    An outcast though he be
  From the haunts where the sun of his childhood
        smil'd,
    And the country of the free:
  Pour the hope of Heaven o'er his desert wild,
    For what home on earth has he?

3 Light for the hills of Greece!
    Light for that trampled clime,
  Where the rage of the spoiler refused to cease
    Ere it wrecked the boast of time:
  If the Moslem hath dealt the gift of peace,
    Can ye grudge your boon sublime?

4   Light on the Hindoo shed!
       On the maddening idol train;
The flame of the suttee is dire and red,
       And the fakir faints with pain;
And the dying moan on their cheerless bed,
       By the Ganges laved in vain.

5   Light for the ancient race
       Exil'd from Zion's rest!
Homeless they roam from place to place,
       Benighted and oppress'd;
They shudder at Sinai's fearful base,—
       Guide them to Calvary's breast.

XXXII.

"It is well."—2 Kings iv. 26.

1 BELOVED, "it is well!"
       God's ways are always right;
    And love is o'er them all,
       Tho' far above our sight.

2 Beloved, "it is well!"
       Tho' deep and sore the smart,

He wounds, who knows to bind
And heal the broken heart.

3 Beloved, " it is well!"
Tho' sorrow clouds our way,
'Twill make the joy more dear
That ushers in the day.

4 Beloved, " it is well!"
The path that Jesus trod,
Tho' rough and dark it be,
Leads home to Heaven and God.

XXXIII.

"And thou Solomon, my son, know thou the God of thy father."—1 Chron. xxviii. 9.

1 My son, know thou the Lord,
Thy father's God obey;
Seek his protecting care by night,
His guiding hand by day.

2 Call while he may be found,
And seek him while he's near;
Serve him with all thy heart and mind,
And worship him in fear.

3 If thou wilt seek his face,
   His ear will hear thy cry;
Then shalt thou find his mercy sure,
   His grace for ever nigh.

XXXIV.

"While he was yet young, he began to seek after the God of David his father."—2 Chron. xxxiv. 3.

1 Lord, look upon a little child,
By nature sinful, rude, and wild;
Oh! put thy gracious hands on me,
And make me all I ought to be.

2 Make me thy child—a child of God,
Wash'd in my Saviour's precious blood;
And my whole soul, from sin set free,
A little vessel full of thee.

3 A star of early dawn, and bright,
Shining within thy sacred light;
A beam of grace to all around,
A little spot of hallow'd ground.

4 Oh! Jesus, take me to thy breast,
And bless me, that I may be blest;

Both when I wake, and when I sleep,
Thy little lamb in safety keep.

XXXV.

"There the weary be at rest."—Job. iii. 17.

1 My Saviour, be thou near me
   Through life's night;
I cry, and thou wilt hear me,—
   Be my light!
My dim sight aching,
Gently thou'rt making
Meet for awaking
   Where all is bright!

2 O, through time's swelling ocean
   Be my guide!
From tempests' wild commotion
   Hide, O hide!
Life's crystal river
Storms ruffle never;
Anchor me ever
   On that calm tide!

XXXVI.

"I would not live alway."—Job vii. 16.

1 What is this life? A constant scene
  Of sighs and tears, of care and pain;
    Moments of sin and months of woe
      Here ebb and flow,
    Till we are summoned hence to go.

2 And what is man? A clod of earth,
  A needy mortal from his birth:
    Brought nothing with him when he came,
      But sin and shame,
    And naked leaves this earthly frame.

3 Evil and few have been my days,
  Weary and sad my pilgrim-ways.
    When God shall call his servant home,
      I'll seek the tomb,
    In hope of endless joys to come.

4 Amen! Thou sovereign God of love
  Grant us thy bliss when we remove;
    That we, redeemed by thy blood,
      May find in God
    Our everlasting sure abode.

XXXVII.

"I know that my Redeemer liveth."—Job. xix. 25.

1 " I know that my Redeemer lives,"
   What comfort that sweet sentence gives!
   He lives! he lives! who once was dead;
   He lives, my Everlasting Head!
   He lives, triumphant from the grave;
   He lives, eternally to save.

2 He lives, all glorious in the sky;
   He lives, exalted there on high;
   He lives, to bless me with his love;
   He lives, to plead my cause above;
   He lives, to upbind and make me whole;
   He lives, to calm my troubled soul.

3 He lives, to grant me rich supply;
   He lives, to guard me with his eye;
   He lives, my hungry soul to feed;
   He lives, to help in time of need;
   He lives, that he may in me dwell;
   He lives, to crush the powers of hell.

4 He lives, to silence all my fears;
  He lives, to stop and dry my tears;
  He lives, my kind, wise, heav'nly friend;
  He lives, and loves me to the end;
  He lives, my Prophet, Priest, and King;
  He lives, and while he lives, I'll sing.

5 He lives, to grant me daily breath;
  He lives, and I shall conquer death;
  He lives, my mansion to prepare;
  He lives, to bring me safely there.
  O, the sweet joy this sentence gives,—
  "I know that my Redeemer lives!"

XXXVIII.

"He knoweth the way that I take."—Job. xxiii. 10.

1 Thy ways, O Lord! with wise design,
    Are framed upon thy throne above;
  And every dark or bending line
    Meets in the centre of thy love.

2 With feeble light, and half obscure,
    Poor mortals thy arrangements view;
  Not knowing that the least are sure,
    The most mysterious just and true.

3 My favour'd soul shall meekly learn
To lay her reason at thy throne :
Too weak thy secrets to discern,
I'll trust thee for my guide alone.

XXXIX.

"Where is God, my Maker, who giveth songs in the night?"—Job xxxv. 10.

1 Sun of my soul! Thou Saviour dear,
It is not night if Thou art near;
Oh, may no earth-born cloud arise
To hide Thee from Thy servant's eyes.

2 When the soft dews of kindly sleep,
My wearied eyelids gently steep,
Be my last thought, how sweet to rest
For ever on my Saviour's breast.

3 Abide with me from morn till eve,
For without Thee I cannot live;
Abide with me when night is nigh,
For without Thee I dare not die.

4 Come near, and bless us when we wake,
  Ere through the world our way we take;
  Till in the ocean of thy love,
  We lose ourselves in Heaven above.

XL.

"O that the salvation of Israel were come out of Zion."—Ps. xiv. 7.

1 In ancient times our fathers made
    Vain gods of wood and stone,
  And all the earth to idols bow'd,
    Save Judah's land alone:
  Around that blest and happy land
    The light of Heaven shone;
  For there the True and Living God
    Had made his statutes known.

2 And Israel's sons, a favoured race,
    Were chosen by the Lord;
  His own peculiar worshippers,—
    The guardians of his word.
  The Lord to them his prophets sent,
    To them his law was given;
  He would have led them as a flock,
    And brought them safe to Heaven.

3 But they rebell'd, and would not fear
  Their own Almighty King;
  They spurn'd the blessings of his love,—
  The shelter of his wing.
  His word, whose deep prophetic tone
  In solemn warning rose,
  Proclaimed in vain the awful truth
  Of Judah's coming woes.

4 And now their land is desolate—
  Their cities overthrown,
  And Israel's wand'ring exil'd sons
  'Mong all the nations sown:
  The light that led their fathers on,
  Shines not around their path;
  For love despis'd and mercy spurn'd,
  Have kindled into wrath.

5 O Lord, incline our hearts to pray
  For Israel's scatter'd race;
  Remove the veil that hides from them
  Their own Messiah's face;
  O banish from their darken'd hearts
  Their unbelief and pride;
  May they behold their promised King
  In Jesus crucified.

6 Thine only is the power, and thine
   The grace that can renew,
In mercy do thou look upon
   The lone and outcast Jew;
Fulfil the promise of thy word,
   Bring the dispers'd again,
Nor let the house of Jacob seek
   Their fathers' God in vain.

7 Oh! when shall Judah's Christian bands
   To Zion's hills return,
And prayer arise like incense sweet,
   And contrite spirits mourn?
Crown'd with her fairest hope, the Church
   Shall glory in her Lord,
And earth her jubilee shall keep
   When Israel is restor'd.

XLI.

"My flesh shall rest in hope."—Ps. xvi. 9.

1 JESUS, I cast my soul on thee,
   Mighty and merciful to save;
Thou wilt to death go down with me,
   And gently lay me in the grave.

2 This body then shall rest in hope,—
   This body which the worms destroy;
   For surely thou wilt bring me up
   To glorious life and endless joy.

XLII.

"Show thy marvellous loving-kindness."—Ps. xvii. 7.

1 Teach me yet more of thy blest ways,
   Thou Holy Lamb of God;
   And fix and root me in the grace,
   So dearly bought with blood.

2 O tell me often of each wound,
   Of every grief and pain;
   And let my heart with joy confess,
   From hence comes all my gain.

3 For this, O may I freely count
   Whate'er I have but loss;
   And every name, and every thing,
   Compar'd with Thee, but dross.

4 Engrave this deeply on my heart
   With an eternal pen;
   That I may, in some small degree,
   Return Thy love again.

XLIII.

"As for me, I will behold thy face in righteousness."—Ps. xvii. 15.

1 Far from these narrow scenes of night,
    Unbounded glories rise,
And realms of infinite delight,
    Unseen by mortal eyes.

2 There pain and sickness never come,
    And griefs no more complain;
And all who reach that peaceful home
    With Jesus ever reign.

3 No cloud these happy regions know,
    For ever bright and fair;
For sin, the source of mortal woe,
    Can never enter there.

4 There no alternate night is known,
    Nor sun's imperfect ray,
But glory from the sacred throne
    Spreads everlasting day.

5 Fair distant land, could now our eyes
    But half its charms explore,
    How would our spirits long to rise
    And dwell on earth no more.

6 Oh, may the heav'nly vision fire
    Our hearts with ardent love,
    Till wings of faith and strong desire
    Bear ev'ry thought above.

XLIV.

"My God will enlighten my darkness."—Ps. xviii. 28.

1 Why fear the path of grief to tread?
    Why, Father, shrink from thy decree?
    If thus my longing soul be led
    A safer, shorter way to thee?

2 On wings of faith, o'er fogs of earth,
    Thy servant, Father, teach to rise,
    And view the blessing's native worth,
    Clear'd from affliction's dark disguise.

3 Yon clouds, a mass of sable shade
    To mortals gazing from below,
  By angels from above survey'd,
    With universal sunshine glow.

XLV.

"I am a worm, and no man."—Ps. xxii. 6.

1 Art thou a child of tears,
    Cradled in care and woe,
  And seems it hard thy vernal years
    Few vernal joys can show?

2 And fall the sounds of mirth
    Sad on thy lonely heart,
  From all the hopes and charms of earth
    Untimely called to part?

3 Look here, and hold thy peace:
    The Giver of all good
  Even from the womb takes no release
    From suffering, tears, and blood.

4 If thou wouldst reap in love,
    First sow in holy fear;
  So life a winter's morn may prove
    To a bright endless year.

XLVI.

"He hath done this!"—Ps. xxii. 31.

1 Glory unto Jesus be!
From the curse he set us free:
All our guilt on Him was laid,
He the ransom fully paid.

2 All his glorious work is done;
God's well pleased in his Son;
For he rais'd him from the dead:
Christ now reigns, the Church's Head.

3 His redeem'd his praise show forth,
Ever glorying in his worth;
Angels sing around the throne,—
"Thou art worthy, thou alone!"

4 Ye who love him, cease to mourn,
He will certainly return;
All his saints with him shall reign;
Come, Lord Jesus, come! Amen.

XLVII.

"Though I walk through the valley of the shadow of death, yet will I fear no evil."—Ps. xxiii. 4.

1 When the spark of life is waning,
   Weep not for me:
When the languid eye is straining,
   Weep not for me:
When the feeble pulse is ceasing,
Start not at its swift decreasing:
'Tis the fetter'd soul's releasing:
   Weep not for me.

2 When the pangs of death assail me,
   Weep not for me:
Christ is mine,—He cannot fail me,
   Weep not for me:
Yes, though sin and doubt endeavour
From his love my soul to sever,
Jesus is my strength for ever!
   Weep not for me.

XLVIII.

"My times are in thy hand."—Ps. xxxi. 15.

1 "My times are in thy hand,"
My God! I wish them there;
My life, my friends, my soul I leave,
Entirely to thy care.

2 "My times are in thy hand,"
Whatever they may be;
Pleasing or painful, dark or bright,
As best may seem to Thee.

3 "My times are in thy hand,"
Why should I doubt or fear?
My Father's hand will never cause
His child a needless tear.

4 "My times are in thy hand,"—
Jesus the crucified!
The hand my cruel sins had pierced
Is now my guard and guide.

5 "My times are in thy hand,"
I'll always trust in thee;
And after death, at thy right hand
I shall for ever be.

XLIX.

*"They looked unto Him and were lightened."—
Ps. xxxiv. 5.*

1 Sweet the moments, rich in blessing,
    Which before the Cross I spend;
  Life and health and peace possessing
    From the sinner's dying friend.

2 Here I'll sit, for ever viewing
    Mercy's streams, in streams of blood;
  Precious drops! my soul bedewing,
    Plead and claim my peace with God,

3 Truly blessed is this station,
    Low before his Cross to lie,
  While I see Divine compassion
    Floating in his languid eye.

4 Here it is I find my Heaven,
    While upon the Cross I gaze;
  Love I much? I'm more forgiven;
    I'm a miracle of grace.

5 Love and grief my heart dividing,
   With my tears his feet I'll bathe;
  Constant still in faith abiding,
   Life deriving from his death.

6 May I still enjoy this feeling,
   In all need to Jesus go ;
  Prove his wounds each day more healing,
   And himself more fully know.

L.

" In thy light shall we see light."—Ps. xxxvi. 9.

1 CHRIST whose glory fills the skies,
   Christ the true, the only Light ;
  Sun of Righteousness arise,
   Triumph o'er the shades of night ;
  Day-spring from on high, be near ;
  Day-star in my heart appear.

2 Dark and cheerless is the morn,
   Unaccompanied by Thee ;
  Joyless is the day's return,
   Till thy mercy's beams I see ;

Till they inward light impart,
Glad my eyes, and warm my heart.

3 Visit, then, this soul of mine,
  Pierce the gloom of sin and grief;
Fill me, Radiancy Divine!
  Scatter all my unbelief:
More and more Thyself display,
Shining to the perfect day.

LI.

"Delight thyself in the Lord."—Ps. xxxvii. 4.

1 O Lord, I would delight in Thee,
    And on thy love depend;
  To thee in every trouble flee,
    My best, my only friend.

2 No good in creatures can be found,
    But may be found in Thee;
  I must have all things and abound,
    While God is God to me.

3 He that has made my Heaven secure
    Will here all good provide;
  While Christ is rich, can I be poor?
    What can I want beside?

4 O Lord, I cast my care on Thee,
I triumph and adore ;
Henceforth my great concern shall be
To love and praise Thee more.

LII.

"I am poor and needy, yet the Lord thinketh on me."—Ps. xl. 17.

1 Poor and needy though I be,
God Almighty cares for me ;
Gives me clothing, shelter, food,—
Gives me all I have of good.

2 He will hear me when I pray,—
He is with me night and day ;
When I sleep, and when I wake,
For the Lord my Saviour's sake.

3 He who reigns above the sky
Once became as poor as I ;
He whose blood for me was shed,
Had not where to lay his head.

4 Though I labour here awhile,
Father, bless me with thy smile ;

And, when this short life is past,
May I rest with Thee at last.

5 Then to Thee I'll tune my song,
Happy as the day is long;
This my joy for ever be,—
God Almighty cares for me.

LIII.

"My soul thirsteth for God."—Ps. xlii. 2.

1 I THIRST, but not as once I did,
    The vain delights of earth to share ;
Thy wounds, Emmanuel, all forbid
    That I should seek my pleasures there.

2 It was the sight of thy dear Cross
    First weaned my soul from earthly things !
And taught me to esteem as dross
    The mirth of fools and pomp of kings.

3 I want that grace that springs from thee,
    That quickens all things where it flows,
And makes a wretched thorn like me
    Bloom as the myrtle, or the rose.

LIV.

"Thou art fairer than the children of men."—Ps. xlv. 2.

1 Jesus, and shall it ever be,
  A mortal man ashamed of Thee?
  Ashamed of Thee, whom angels praise,
  Whose glory shines through endless days!

2 Ashamed of Jesus! sooner far
  Let evening blush to own a star!
  He sheds his beams of light divine
  On this benighted soul of mine.

3 Ashamed of Jesus! just as soon
  Let midnight be ashamed of noon;
  'Tis midnight with my soul, till He,
  Bright morning star, bids darkness flee.

4 Ashamed of Jesus! that dear friend,
  On whom my hopes of Heaven depend!
  No! when I blush, be this my shame,
  That I no more revere His name.

5 Ashamed of Jesus! yes, I may,
  When I've no guilt to wash away,

No fears to quell, no good to crave,
And no immortal soul to save.

6 Till then,—nor is my boasting vain,—
Till then, I boast a Saviour slain;
And, O, may this my glory be,
That Christ is not ashamed of me.

LV.

"There is a river, the streams whereof shall make glad the city of our God."—Ps. xlvi. 4.

1 CLEAR Spring of Life! flow on and roll
With growing swell from pole to pole,
Till flowers and fruits of Paradise
Round all thy winding current rise!

2 Still near thy stream may I be found,
Long as I tread this earthly ground!
Cheer with thy wave death's gloomy shade,
Then thro' the fields of Canaan spread.

LVI.

"God is gone up with a shout."—Ps. xlvii. 5.

1 Go up with shouts of praise!
    Go up, High-priest, to Heaven,
Who hast the ransom'd race
    Upon thy heart engraven;
Though seated on thy throne,
    Thou deign'st to hear our pray'r,
Nor art ashamed to own
    That we thy brethren are.

LVII.

"Open thou my lips, and my mouth shall show forth thy praise."—Ps. li. 15.

1 COME, thou Fount of every blessing,
    Tune my heart to sing thy grace:
Streams of mercy, never ceasing,
    Call for songs of loudest praise.

2 Here I raise my Ebenezer,
    Hither by thy help I'm come;
And I hope, by thy good pleasure,
    Safely to arrive at home.

3 Jesus sought me when a stranger,
    Wandering from the fold of God;
  He, to save my soul from danger,
    Interpos'd his precious blood.

4 Oh! to grace how great a debtor
    Daily I'm constrain'd to be!
  Let that grace, Lord, like a fetter,
    Bind my wandering heart to thee.

5 Prone to wander, Lord, I feel it;
    Prone to leave the God of love:
  Here's my heart, Lord, take and seal it,
    Seal it from thy courts above.

LVIII.

"I would hasten my escape from the windy storm and tempest."—Ps. lv. 8.

1 Here I find no rest;
    By fierce pain opprest,
    And by sin distrest,
        I am weary, weary!

2 Though this world be fair,
    Sin is ever there,

And its guilt I share :
    I am weary, weary!

3 Soon death's night will come,—
Where is now the gloom
Of the silent tomb?
    I am weary, weary!

4 Christ hath died to prove
God's amazing love,
Oh for life above!
    I am weary, weary!

5 Earth gives me no pleasure;
Heaven contains my treasure,—
Bliss in boundless measure :
    I am weary, weary!

6 Why should I complain?
Jesus suffer'd pain,
And for me was slain:
    I am weary, weary!

7 Now, from Heaven on high,
Christ hath heard my sigh,
Mark'd my mournful cry :
    I am weary, weary!

8 He hath given me peace,
  Even tho' pains increase,
  Soon shall sorrow cease:
    I am weary, weary!

9 Dawn, thou Heav'nly light,
  On my vanished sight;
  All there's pure and bright!
    I am weary, weary!

LIX.

"Oh, that I had wings like a dove: I would fly away and be at rest."—Ps. lv. 6.

1 My soul, amid this stormy world,
    Is like some flutter'd dove;
  And fain would be as swift of wing,
    To flee to Him I love.

2 The cords that bound my heart to earth
    Are broken by his hand:
  Before his cross I found myself,
    A stranger in the land.

3 That visage marr'd, those sorrows deep,
    The vinegar and gall,

Were Jesus' golden chains of love
His captive to enthral!

4 My heart is with Him on His throne,
And ill can brook delay;
Each moment list'ning for the voice,—
"Rise up, and come away."

5 With hope deferr'd, oft sick and faint,
"Why tarries he?" I cry:
And should my Saviour chide my haste,
Sure I could make reply.

6 May not an exile, Lord, desire,
His own sweet land to see?
May not a captive seek release,—
A pris'ner to be free?

7 A child, when far away, may long
For home and kindred dear;
And she that wails her absent Lord
May sigh till he appear.

8 I would, my Lord and Saviour, know,
That which no measure knows;
Would search the mystery of thy love,—
The depth of all thy woes.

LX.

"My soul followeth hard after Thee: Thy right hand upholdeth me."—Ps. lxiii. 8.

1 We go with the redeem'd to taste
    Of joy supreme, that never dies;
  Our feet still press the weary waste,
    Our hearts, our home, are in the skies.

2 And oh! while on to Zion's hill
    The toilsome path of life we tread,
  Around us, loving Father, still
    Thy circling wings of mercy spread.

3 From day to day, from hour to hour,
    Oh! let our rising spirits prove
  The strength of thine Almighty pow'r,
    The sweetness of thy saving love.

LXI.

"His name shall endure for ever: men shall be blessed in Him: all nations shall call Him blessed."—Ps. lxxii. 17.

1 Jesus shall reign where'er the sun
    Does his successive journies run;

His kingdom stretch from shore to shore,
Till moons shall wax and wane no more.

2 For him shall endless prayer be made,
And ceaseless praises crown his head ;
His name like sweet perfume shall rise
With ev'ry morning sacrifice.

3 People and realms of ev'ry tongue
Dwell on his love with sweetest song ;
And infant voices shall proclaim
Their early blessings on his name.

4 Blessings abound where'er he reigns,
The pris'ner leaps to lose his chains,
The weary find eternal rest,
And all the sons of want are blest.

5 Where he displays his healing pow'r,
Death and the curse are known no more,
In him the tribes of Adam boast
More blessings than their father lost.

6 Let ev'ry creature rise, and bring
Peculiar honours to our King ;
Angels descend with songs again,
And earth repeat the loud Amen.

LXII.

"I am continually with thee."—Ps. lxxiii. 23.

1 Oh Thou, by long experience tried,
  Near whom no grief can long abide;
  My Lord, how full of sweet content
  I pass my years of banishment!

2 All scenes alike engaging prove
  To souls impress'd with sacred love!
  Where'er they dwell, they dwell in Thee;
  In Heaven, in earth, or on the sea.

3 To me remains nor place nor time,
  My country is in every clime;
  I can be calm and free from care
  On any shore, since God is there.

4 While place we seek, or place we shun,
  The soul finds happiness in none;
  But with a God to guide our way,
  'Tis equal joy to go or stay.

5 Could I be cast where Thou art not,
  That were indeed a dreadful lot;
  But regions none remote I call,
  Secure of finding God in all.

LXIII.

"Thou shalt guide me with Thy counsel, and afterwards receive me to glory."—Ps. lxxiii. 24.

1 When the vale of death appears,
   Faint and cold this mortal clay,
Kind Forerunner, soothe my fears,
   Light me through the darksome way:
      Break the shadows,
   Usher in eternal day.

2 Starting from this dying state.
   Upward bid my soul aspire;
Open thou the crystal gate,
   To thy praise attune my lyre:
      Dwell for ever,—
   Dwell on each immortal wire.

3 From the sparkling turrets there,
   Oft I'll trace my pilgrim way;
Often bless thy guardian care,—
   Fire by night, and cloud by day,—
      While my triumphs
   At my Leader's feet I lay.

3 And when mighty trumpets blown
    Shall the judgment dawn proclaim,
From the central burning throne,
    'Mid creation's final flame,
        With the ransom'd,
Judge and Saviour, own my name!

LXIV.

"How amiable are thy tabernacles, O Lord of Hosts."—Ps. lxxxiv. 1.

1 LORD of the worlds above,
    How pleasant and how fair
The dwellings of thy love,
    Thy earthly temples are!
    To thine abode
      My heart aspires,
      With warm desires
    To see my God.

2 O happy souls that pray
    Where God appoints to hear!
O happy men that pay
    Their constant service there!

They praise thee still;
And happy they
That love the way
To Zion's hill.

3 They go from strength to strength,
Through this dark vale of tears,
Till each arrives at length,—
Till each in Heaven appears.
O glorious seat,
When God our King
Shall thither bring
Our willing feet.

LXV.

"My soul longeth, yea, even fainteth for the courts of the Lord."—Ps. lxxxiv. 2.

1 For thee we long and pray,
O blessed Sabbath morn!
And all the week we say,
O! when wilt thou return!
Come, come away,
Day of glad rest,
Of days the best,
Sweet Sabbath day!

2 Thou tellest us how Christ
　　Arose and left the tomb;
　And all the week we say,
　　O! when will Sabbath come?
　　Come, come away, &c.

3 Thou tellest us how we,
　　Like Him, shall leave the tomb:
　And all the week we say,
　　O! when will Sabbath come?
　　Come, come, away, &c.

4 Thou tellest of a rest,—
　　A peaceful happy home,
　Where all the saints are blest:
　　O! when will Sabbath come?
　　Come, come away, &c.

LXVI.

"They go from strength to strength; every one of them in Zion appeareth before God."—Ps. lxxxiv. 7.

1 STILL in a world of sin and pain,
　Far from our home, we meet again;
　Dreary and long our course may be,
　But oh, our God, it leads to thee;

Thou art the light by which we roam,—
Thou art our everlasting home.

2 Thy hand is still around to bless,
Thou dost not leave us comfortless;
Earth and its pain we still may feel,
But Thou art ever near to heal;
Still as our day our strength shall be,
For all our cares are borne by Thee.

3 Still, as time's changing current rolls,
Thy comforts, Lord, delight our souls;
Thy mighty arm to smooth our way,
Thy light to turn our night to day;
Onward with firmer steps we roam,
On to our everlasting home.

LXVII.

"A day in thy courts is better than a thousand."
Ps. lxxxiv. 10.

1 Welcome, sweet day of rest,
That saw the Lord arise;
Welcome to this reviving breast,
And these rejoicing eyes!

2 The King himself comes near,
   And feasts his saints to-day;
Here we may sit, and see him here,
   And love, and praise, and pray.

3 One day amidst the place
   Where my dear God hath been,
Is sweeter than ten thousand days
   Of pleasurable sin.

4 My willing soul would stay
   In such a frame as this,
And sit and sing herself away
   To everlasting bliss.

LXVIII.

"All my springs are in Thee."—Ps. lxxxvii. 7.

1 Bliss beyond compare,
   Which in Christ I share!
He's my only joy and treasure;
Tasteless is all worldly pleasure,
   When in Christ I share
   Bliss beyond compare.

2   Jesus is my joy,
    Therefore, blest am I.
    O! his mercy is unbounded,
    All my hope on him is founded;
    Jesus is my joy,
    Therefore, blest am I.

3   When the Lord appears,
    This my spirit cheers;
    When, his love to me revealing,
    He, the Sun of Grace, with healing,
    In his beams appears,—
    This my spirit cheers.

4   Then all grief is drown'd;
    Pure delight is found.
    Joy and peace in his salvation,
    Heav'nly bliss and consolation.
    Ev'ry grief is drown'd
    Where such bliss is found.

LXIX.

"From everlasting to everlasting Thou art God."
Ps. xc. 2.

1 How long sometimes a day appears,
   And weeks, how long are they!
Months move as slow as if the years
   Would never pass away!

2 But months and years are passing by,
   And soon must all be gone;
For day by day as minutes fly,
   Eternity comes on.

3 Days, months, and years must have an end,
   Eternity has none;
It never can its ages spend,
   Even as they ne'er begun.

4 Great God! an infant cannot tell
   How such a thing can be;
I only pray that I may dwell
   That long, long time with thee.

LXX.

"He that dwelleth in the secret place of the Most High shall abide under the shadow of the Almighty."—Ps. xci. 1.

1 CALL Jehovah thy salvation,
   Rest beneath the Almighty's shade,
In his secret habitation
   Dwell, nor ever be dismay'd;
There no tumult can alarm thee,
   Thou shalt dread no hidden snare;
Guile nor violence can harm thee,
   In eternal safeguard there.

2 From the sword, at noon-day wasting,
   From the noisome pestilence,
In the depth of midnight blasting,
   God shall be thy sure defence.
Fear not thou the deadly quiver,
   When a thousand feel the blow,
Mercy shall thy soul deliver,
   Though ten thousand be laid low.

3 Thee, though winds and waves be swelling,
   God, thine hope, shall bear through all,

Plague shall not come near thy dwelling,
   Thee no evil shall befall;
He shall charge his angel-legions
   Watch and guard o'er thee to keep,
Though thou walk through hostile regions,
   Though in desert wilds thou sleep.

4 Since, with pure and true affection,
   Thou on God has set thy love,
With the wings of his protection
   He will shield thee from above:
Thou shalt call on him in trouble,
   He will hearken, he will save;
Here for grief reward thee double,
   Crown with life beyond the grave.

LXXI.

"My God is the Rock of my refuge."—Ps. xciv. 22.

1 Rock of Ages, cleft for me,
   Let me hide myself in thee;
Let the water and the blood,
   From thy wounded side which flow'd,
Be of sin the double cure;
   Cleanse me from its guilt and power.

2 Not the labor of my hands
Can fulfil thy law's demands;
Could my zeal no respite know,
Could my tears for ever flow,
All for sin could not atone;
Thou must save, and thou alone.

3 Nothing in my hand I bring,
Simply to thy Cross I cling;
Naked come to thee for dress;
Helpless, look to thee for grace;
Guilty, to the fountain fly;
Wash me, Saviour, or I die!

4 While I draw this fleeting breath,
When my eyes are clos'd in death,
When I soar to worlds unknown,
See Thee on thy judgment throne:
Rock of Ages, cleft for me,
Let me hide myself in Thee.

LXXII.

"Let the heavens rejoice and let the earth be glad before the Lord, for He cometh."—Ps. xcvi. 11.

1 Songs of praise the angels sang
   Heaven with hallelujah's rang,
   When Jehovah's work began,—
   When He spake, and it was done.

2 Songs of praise awoke the morn
   When the Prince of Peace was born;
   Songs of praise arose when He
   Captive led captivity.

3 Heaven and earth must pass away,
   Songs of praise shall crown the day:
   God will make new heavens and earth,
   Songs of praise shall hail their birth.

4 And shall man alone be dumb
   Till that glorious kingdom come?
   No! the Church is called to raise
   Psalms and hymns and songs of praise.

5 Learning thus, by faith and love,
Songs of praise to sing above:
Soon this holy sweet employ
She in glory shall enjoy.

LXXIII.

"Bless the Lord, O my soul, and all that is within me, bless His holy name."—Ps. ciii. 1.

1 LET sinners sav'd give thanks and sing
Of mercies past, of joys to come;
The Lord their Saviour is, and King,
The Cross their hope, and Heav'n their home.

2 Let sinners sav'd give thanks and sing,—
Sweet is the subject of their song;
Who made the children of a King
Expect to sit in Heav'n ere long.

3 Let sinners sav'd give thanks and sing,—
The Lord has kept in dangers past;
And oh, sweet thought, the Lord will bring
His people safe to Heav'n at last!

4 Let sinners sav'd, give thanks and sing,
Of Jesus sing through all their days;

In Heav'n their golden harps they'll string,
And there for ever sing His praise.

LXXIV.

"For my love they are my adversaries; they rewarded me hatred for my love."—Ps. cix. 4–5.

1 WHAT grace, O Lord, and beauty shone
  Around thy steps below;
What patient love was seen in all
  Thy life and death of woe.

2 For ever on thy burden'd heart
  A weight of sorrow hung,
Yet no ungentle murm'ring word
  Escaped thy silent tongue.

3 Thy foes might hate, despise, revile,—
  Thy friends unfaithful prove;
Unwearied in forgiveness still,
  Thy heart could only love.

4 O give us hearts to love like thee,—
  Like thee, O Lord, to grieve
Far more for others' sins than all
  The wrongs that we receive.

5 One with thyself, may every eye
　In us, thy brethren, see
That gentleness and grace that spring
　From union, Lord, with Thee.

LXXV.

"I am thine, save me, for I have sought Thy precepts."—Ps. cxix. 94.

1 To Thee my heart would tell its griefs, O Lord,
　My burning tears into thy bosom flow,
For thou hast promised, in thy faithful Word
　That thou wilt bear the weight of all my woe.

2 And I am thine! O that my life were spent
　In doing only all thy righteous will;
That I might walk, on holiness intent,
　And every hour delight to love Thee still.

3 Yes, I with joy from every sin would flee,
　Nor for a moment should my heart delay;
But speak the word, and that one word from Thee
　I would with willingness at once obey.

4 When shall the hour of my deliverance be?
　When shall the law of death no more remain?

When my dear Saviour shall I joyful see,—
Thy love alone within my bosom reign?

5 Till that blest day, thy aid would I entreat,
Inspire me as the conflict I renew;
My safety is in thee—thy work complete:
O, be my Rock, and my Redeemer too!

LXXVI.

"O how love I thy law."—Ps. cxix. 97.

1 Holy Bible! book divine!
Precious treasure! thou art mine.
Mine, to tell me whence I came;
Mine, to teach me what I am:

2 Mine, to chide me when I rove;
Mine, to show a Saviour's love:
Mine art thou, to guide my feet;
Mine, to judge, condemn, acquit:

3 Mine, to comfort in distress,
If the Holy Spirit bless:
Mine to show, by living faith,
How to triumph over death!

4 Mine, to tell of joys to come,
And the rebel-sinner's doom :—
O thou precious book divine!
Precious treasure! thou art mine.

LXXVII.

"O how I love thy law; it is my meditation all the day."—Ps. cxix. 97.

1 PRECIOUS book! of books the best,
Dearest gift of God, but one
That surpasses all the rest,—
Gift of God's beloved Son,
Gracious Spirit—heavenly Dove,
Thee I'd slight not, Thee I'd love,
By thy power, and thine alone,
The value of this gift I've known.

LXXVIII.

"Order my steps in Thy word, and let not any iniquity have dominion over me."—Ps. cxix. 133.

1 THOU who didst, for Peter's faith,
Kindly condescend to pray;

Thou, whose loving-kindness hath
  Kept me to the present day:
    Kind Conductor!
  Still direct my devious way.

2 When a tempting world in view
    Gains upon my yielding heart,—
  When its pleasures I pursue,
    Then one look of pity dart;
      Teach me pleasures
    Which the world can ne'er impart.

3 When, with horrid thoughts profane,
    Satan would my soul invade;
  When he calls religion vain,
    Mighty Victor! be my aid!
      Send thy Spirit,—
    Bid me conflict undismay'd.

4 When my unbelieving fear
    Makes me think myself too vile,—
  When the legal curse I hear,
    Cheer me with a gospel smile;
      Or if hiding,
    Hide thee only for a while.

5 When I sit beneath thy word,
　At thy table cold and dead,
　When I cannot see my Lord,
　All my little day-light fled,—
　　Sun of Glory,
　Beam again around my head.

6 When thy statutes I forsake,
　When thy graces dimly shine,
　When the covenant I break,
　Jesus, then remember thine!
　　Check my wanderings
　By a look of love divine.

7 Then, if heavenly dews distil,
　If my hopes are bright and clear,
　While I sit on Zion's hill,
　Temper joy with holy fear;
　　Keep me watchful,—
　Safe alone when Thou art near.

8 When afflictions cloud my sky,
　When the tide of sorrow flows,
　When thy rod is lifted high,
　Let me on thy love repose;

Stay thy rough wind
When thy chilling eastern blows.

LXXIX.

"Rivers of waters run down mine eyes, because they keep not thy law."—Ps. cxix. 136.

1 Arise, my tend'rest thoughts arise;
  To torrents melt, my streaming eyes;
  And thou, my heart, with anguish feel
  Those evils which thou canst not heal.

2 See human nature sunk in shame;
  See scandals pour'd on Jesus' name;
  The Father wounded thro' the Son;
  The world abus'd, the soul undone.

3 See the short course of vain delight
  Closing in everlasting night;
  In flames that no abatement know,
  Tho' bitter tears for ever flow.

4 My God, I feel the mournful scene;
  My bowels yearn o'er dying men;
  And fain my pity would reclaim
  And snatch the firebrands from the flame.

5 But feeble my compassion proves,
   And can but weep where most it loves :
   Thine own all-saving arm employ,
   And turn these drops of grief to joy.

LXXX.

"So He giveth His beloved sleep."—Ps. cxxvii. 2.

1 INTERVAL of grateful shade,
  Welcome to my weary head !
  Welcome slumbers to my eyes—
  Tired with glaring vanities !
  My great Master still allows
  Needful periods of repose.

2 By my heavenly Father blest,
  Thus I give my powers to rest,
  Heavenly Father ! gracious name !
  Night and day His love the same.
  Far be each suspicious thought,
  Every anxious care forgot.

3 Thou, my ever bounteous God,
  Crown'st my days with various good ;
  Thy kind eye, that cannot sleep,

These defenceless hours shall keep.
Blest vicissitude to me,
Day and night I'm still with thee!

LXXXI.

"Surely I have behaved and quieted myself as a child that is weaned of his mother."—Ps. cxxxi. 2.

1 As a little weaned child,
   Holy Saviour, may I be:
Humble, teachable, and mild,—
   Altogether like to Thee.

2 While king David was a man,
   Still he prayed to be a child;
And king David's Saviour can
   Make me humble, meek, and mild.

3 When king David was a king,
   While he sat on Israel's throne,
He was not too proud to sing
   Praises to the Lord alone.

4 Surely, then, a child like me
   Never should be proud in heart:

Lord, thy grace is rich and free,—
Grace like his to me impart.

5 Give me, Lord, such heavenly love,
As thou didst to Israel's king,
Then, where David sings above,
I, ere long, shall also sing.

LXXXII.

ANOTHER OF THE SAME.

1 QUIET, Lord, my froward heart,
Make me teachable and mild,
Upright, simple, free from art.
Make me as a weaned child :
From distrust and envy free,
Pleas'd with all that pleases Thee.

2 What thou shalt to-day provide,
Let me as a child receive ;
What to-morrow may betide,
Calmly to thy wisdom leave ;
'Tis enough that Thou wilt care,
Why should I the burden bear?

3 As a little child relies
   On a care beyond his own;
Knows he's neither strong nor wise;
   Fears to stir a step alone;
     Let me thus with thee abide,
     As my Father, Guard, and Guide.

4 Thus preserv'd from Satan's wiles,
   Safe from dangers, free from fears,
May I live upon thy smiles,
   Till the promis'd hour appears,
     When the sons of God shall prove
     All their Father's boundless love.

LXXXIII.

"My soul is even as a weaned child."—Ps. cxxxi. 2.

1 Act but the infant's gentle part;
Give up to love thy willing heart,
No fondest parent's melting breast
Yearns like thy God's to make thee blest.
Taught its dear mother soon to know,
The tenderest babe its love can show;
Bid thy base slavish fear retire,—
This task no labor will require.

2 Thy heavenly Father, good and kind,
Wants but to have his child resign'd;
Wants but thy yielded heart, no more!
With his large gifts of grace to store.
Thy gentle Father, best of friends,
To thee, nor loss, nor harm intends;
Though tost on a tempestuous main,
No wreck thy vessel shall sustain.

3 On His sure, faithful arm divine,
Firm let thy fastening trust recline;
Sweet light shall from the tranquil skies
Like a fair dawn before thee rise.
Come, backward soul, to God resign!
Peace, his best blessing, shall be thine,
Boldly reclining on his care,
Cast all thy burdens only there.

LXXXIV.

" O give thanks unto the Lord, for He is good, for His mercy endureth for ever."—Ps. cxxxvi. 1.

1 Praise to thee thou great Creator,
　Praise be thine from ev'ry tongue;
　Join my soul, with ev'ry creature,—
　Join the universal song.

2 For ten thousand blessings given,
  For the richest gifts bestowed,
  Sound His praise thro' earth and heaven,—
  Sound Jehovah's praise abroad.

LXXXV.

"O give thanks unto the God of heaven; for his mercy endureth for ever."—Ps. cxxxvi. 26.

1 Let us, with a gladsome mind,
  Praise the Lord, for He is kind;
  For His mercies shall endure,—
  Ever faithful, ever sure.

2 He, with all-commanding might,
  Fill'd the new-made world with light:
  For His mercies shall endure,—
  Ever faithful, ever sure.

3 All things living he doth feed:
  His full hand supplies their need:
  For His mercies shall endure,—
  Ever faithful, ever sure.

4 He His chosen race did bless
  In the wasteful wilderness:

For His mercies shall endure,—
Ever faithful, ever sure.

5 He hath, with a piteous eye,
Look'd upon our misery:
For His mercies shall endure,—
Ever faithful, ever sure.

LXXXVI.

" Sing us one of the songs of Zion."—Ps. cxxxvii. 3.

1 Sing them, my children, sing them still,
Those sweet and holy songs!
Oh, let the psalms of Zion hill
Be heard from youthful tongues.
Oh, sing them at the cheerful dawn,
The rising morn to cheer;
And sing them round the evening hearth,
When fires are blazing clear.

2 Sing them when Sabbath schools are met,
And your young voices raise
Their Sabbath-evening melodies
To their Redeemer's praise.
So shall each unforgotten word,
When distant far you roam,

Call back your hearts which once it stirred,
  To childhood's blessed home.

3 Sing them, my children; many a saint
    These holy strains has sung!
  These hills of ours have echoed them
    From many a martyr's tongue.
  Oh, sing them in a land like this,
    Where martyrs' steps have rov'd;
  My children, sing those melodies,—
    The songs our fathers loved!

LXXXVII.

"When I awake I am still with thee."—Ps. cxxxix. 18.

1 My God was with me all this night,
    And gave me sweet repose;
  My God did watch, even while I slept,
    Or I had never rose.
  What ills have I escaped this night,
    Which have on others fell!
  My body might have slept its last,
    My soul have waked in hell.

2 Lord, for the mercies of the night,
    My humble thanks I pay,
And unto Thee I dedicate
    The first-fruits of the day.
Let this day praise Thee, O my God,
    And so let all my days;
And O, let mine eternal day
    Be thine eternal praise.

LXXXVIII.

"Praise ye the Lord, both young men and maidens, old men and children."—Ps. cxlviii. 12.

1 GLORY to the Father give;
God, in whom we move and live;
Children's prayers he deigns to hear;
Children's songs delight his ear.

2 Glory to the Son we bring,
Christ our Prophet, Priest, and King;
Children, raise your sweetest strain
To the Lamb, for He was slain.

3 Glory to the Holy Ghost—
Be this day a Pentecost—

Children's minds may He inspire,
　　　Touch their tongues with holy fire.

4　Glory in the highest be
　　To the blessed Trinity,
　　For the gospel from above,
　　For the word that " God is love."

LXXXIX.

"Let the children of Zion be joyful in their King."
　　　　　—Ps. cxlix. 2.

1　Ye holy angels bright,
　　　Who stand before God's throne,
　　And dwell in glorious light,
　　　Praise ye the Lord each one!
　　　　You there so nigh,
　　　　　Fitter than we
　　　　　Dark sinners be
　　　　For things so high.

2　You blessed souls at rest,
　　　Who see your Saviour's face,
　　Whose glory, even the least,
　　　Is far above our grace,

God's praises sound,
　　As in His sight,
　　With sweet delight,
You do abound.

3 All nations of the earth,
　　Extol the world's Great King,
With melody and mirth,
　　His glorious praises sing!
　　For He still reigns,
　　　And will bring low
　　The proudest foe
　　　That Him disdains.

4 Sing forth Jehovah's praise,
　　Ye saints that on Him call;
Him magnify always,
　　His holy churches all!
　　In Him rejoice,
　　　And there proclaim
　　His holy name,
　　　With sounding voice.

XC.

"Let every thing that hath breath praise the Lord."
—Ps. cl. 6.

1   Angels holy,
    High and lowly,
Sing the praises of the Lord !
Earth and sky, all living nature,
Man, the stamp of thy Creator,
Praise ye, praise ye, God the Lord !

2   Sun and moon bright,
    Night and noon light,
Starry temples, azure-floored ;
Calm and storm, and wild wind's madness,
Sons of God, that shout for gladness,
Praise ye, praise ye, God the Lord !

3   Rolling thunder,
    Voice of wonder,
Deepest bass in heavenly chord ;
Vivid lightnings fiercely gleaming,
Bulging clouds with water streaming,
Praise ye, praise ye, God the Lord !

4   Ocean hoary,
            Tell his glory,
Cliffs where tumbling seas have roar'd!
Pulse of water, blithely beating,
Wave advancing, wave retreating,
Praise ye, praise ye, God the Lord!

5   Rock and high land,
            Wood and island,
Crag where eagle's pride hath soar'd;
Mighty mountain, purple breasted,
Peaks, cloud-cleaving, snowy-crested,
Praise ye, praise ye, God the Lord!

6   Rolling river,
            Praise him ever,
From the mountain's deep vein poured;
Silver fountain clearly gushing,
Troubled torrent madly rushing,
Praise ye, praise ye, God the Lord!

7   Birds whose pinion
            Gives dominion,
In sky-regions deep and broad;
Flocks that stray o'er hills unbounded,
Herds, with verdant plains surrounded,
Praise ye, praise ye, God the Lord!

8   Youth, whose morning
          Smiles at warning,
Age in counsel deeply stor'd ;
Maids and boys, in chorus blending,
Let your anthem-song, ascending,
Praise high Heaven's eternal Lord!

9   Bond and free men,
          Land and seamen,
Earth, with peoples widely stor'd ;
Woodman, lone, in prairies ample,
Full-voiced choir in costly temple,
Praise ye, praise ye, God the Lord!

10   Kings anointed,
          God-appointed,
Sceptred by the Sovereign Lord ;
Tribes and golden realms possessing,
Throned in grandeur, power, and blessing,
Praise *your* ruler, God the Lord!

11   Spread the story
          Of his glory,
Ye who fiercely scorned His word ;
Israel ! once that outcast nation,
Now, illustrious in salvation,
Praise your Kinsman, King, and Lord !

12   Praise Him ever,
        Bounteous Giver,
Praise Him, Father, Friend, and Lord;
Each glad soul its free course winging—
Each blithe voice its free song singing,
Praise the great, the mighty Lord!

XCI.

"The righteous hath hope in his death."—Prov. xiv. 32.

1 Ah! I shall soon be dying,
    Time swiftly glides away;
  But on my Lord relying,
    I hail the happy day;—

2 The day when I shall enter
    Upon a world unknown;
  My helpless soul I venture
    On Jesus Christ alone.

3 He once a spotless victim
    Upon Mount Calvary bled!
  Jehovah did afflict Him,
    And bruise Him in my stead.

4 Hence all my hope arises,
    Unworthy as I am ;
My soul most surely prizes
    The sin-atoning Lamb.

5 To Him by grace united,
    I joy in Him alone ;
And now, by faith, delighted
    Behold Him on His throne.

6 There He is interceding
    For all who on Him rest :
The grace from Him proceeding
    Shall waft me to His breast.

7 Then, with the saints in glory,
    The grateful song I'll raise,
And chaunt my blissful story
    In high seraphic lays.

8 Free grace, redeeming merit,
    And sanctifying love,
Of Father, Son and Spirit,
    Shall charm the courts above.

XCII.
"The glory of children are their fathers."—Prov. xvii. 6.

1 There was gladness in Zion, her standard was flying,
  Free o'er her battlements, glorious and gay;
  All fair as the morning shone forth her adorning,
  And fearful to foes was her godly array.

2 There is mourning in Zion, her standard is lying,
  Defiled in the dust, to the spoiler a prey;
  And now there is wailing, and sorrow prevailing,
  For the best of her children are weeded away.

3 The good have been taken, their place is forsaken—
  The man and the maiden, the green and the grey;
  The voice of the weepers wails over the sleepers—
  The martyrs of Scotland that now are away.

4 The hue of her waters is crimson'd with slaughters,
  And the blood of the martyrs has redden'd the clay;
  And dark desolation broods over the nation,
  For the faithful are perished, the good are away.

5 On the mountains of heather they slumber together;
  On the wastes of the moorland their bodies decay:
  How sound is their sleeping, how safe is their keeping,
  Though far from their kindred they moulder away!

6 Their blessing shall hover, their children to cover,
  Like the cloud of the desert, by night and by day;
  Oh, never to perish, their names let us cherish,
  The martyrs of Scotland that now are away!

XCIII.

"A friend loveth at all times."—Prov. xvii. 17.

1 One there is, above all others,
    Well deserves the name of friend;
  His is love beyond a brother's,
    Costly, free, and knows no end!
  They who once his kindness prove,
  Find it everlasting love.

2 Which of all our friends, to save us
   Could or would have shed his blood!
But our Jesus died to have us
   Reconcil'd in Him to God:
This was boundless love indeed!
Jesus is a friend in need.

3 When he liv'd on earth abased,
   Friend of sinners was His name;
Now, above all glory raised,
   He rejoices in the same:
Still He calls them brethren, friends,
And to all their wants attends.

4 O, for grace our hearts to soften!
   Teach us, Lord, at length to love:
We, alas, forget too often
   What a friend we have above:
But, when home our souls are brought,
We will love thee as we ought.

XCIV.

"There is a Friend that sticketh closer than a brother."—Prov. xviii. 24.

1 One there is above all others—
   O how He loves!
His is love beyond a brother's—
   O how He loves!
Earthly friends may fail or leave us,
One day soothe, the next day grieve us,
But this Friend will ne'er deceive us—
   O how He loves!

2 'Tis eternal life to know Him—
   O how He loves!
Think, O think how much we owe Him—
   O how He loves!
With His precious blood He bought us,
In the wilderness He sought us,
To His fold He safely brought us—
   O how He loves!

3 We have found a friend in Jesus—
   O how He loves!
'Tis His great delight to bless us—
   O how He loves!

How our hearts delight to hear Him
Bid us dwell in safety near Him:
Why should we distrust or fear Him?—
O how He loves!

4 Through His name we are forgiven—
O how He loves!
Backward shall our foes be driven—
O how He loves!
Best of blessings He'll provide us,
Nought but good shall e'er betide us—
Safe to glory He will guide us—
O HOW HE LOVES!

XCV.

"Thine own friend, and thy father's friend, forsake not."—Prov. xxvii. 10.

1 THINK not that e'er my heart could dwell
   Contented far from thee;
How can the fresh-caught nightingale
   Enjoy tranquillity?

2 Oh, then, forsake thy friend for nought
   That slanderous tongues can say;
The heart that fixes where it ought,
   No power can rend away.

XCVI.

"In her tongue is the law of kindness."—Prov. xxxi. 26.

1 Speak kindly to thy fellow man,
    Lest he should die, while yet
Thy bitter accents wring his heart
    And make his pale cheek wet.

2 Speak to him tenderly ; for he
    Hath many toils to bear ;
And he is weak, and often sighs—
    As thou dost—under care.

3 Speak to him lovingly ; he is
    A brother of thine own :
He well may claim thy sympathies
    Who's bone of thine own bone.

4 Speak to him meekly ; he may be
    A holier man than thou,
And fitting it may be for thee
    To him with reverence bow.

5 Speak to him solemnly ; for thou
    And he must surely meet,

To make account for idle words,
 Before the judgment-seat.

6 Speak to him faithfully; thy word
 May touch him deep within,
 And save his erring soul from death,
 And cover o'er his sin!

XCVII.

"Vanity of vanities, all is vanity."—Eccles. i. 2.

1 Our mortal life will soon be done,
 The tomb now warns us to prepare,—
 Our measured course will soon be run,
 We hasten where our fathers are.
 O vanity of vanities!

2 What real good commands our care,
 Our labours, all our numerous ends?
 At best, but glittering chains we wear,
 Some empty name, some fickle friends,
 O vanity of vanities!

3 Our course of years is speeding fast!
 We touch upon eternity;

O, Jesus, take our souls at last,
And let them cloth'd in glory be!
O wash away our vanities.

XCVIII.

"Draw me, we will run after thee."—Song of Solomon i. 4.

1 O draw me, Saviour, after Thee,
So shall I run, and never tire;
With gracious words still comfort me,
Be Thou my hope, my sole desire.
Free me from every weight; nor fear,
Nor sin can come, if Thou art here.

2 What in thy love possess I not?
My star by night, my sun by day,
My spring of life when parch'd with drought,
My wine to cheer, my bread to stay,
My strength, my shield, my safe abode,
My robe before the throne of God.

3 From all eternity with love
Unchangeable Thou hast me view'd;
Ere knew this beating heart to move,
Thy tender mercies me pursued:

Ever with me may they abide,
And close me in on every side.

4 In suffering, be Thy love my peace,
In weakness, be Thy love my power;
And when the storms of life shall cease,
Jesus, in that important hour,
In death, in life, be Thou my guide,
And save me, who for me hast died!

XCIX.

"He brought me to the banqueting house."—Song ii. 4.

1 WHILE in sweet communion feeding
On this earthly bread and wine,
Saviour, may we see Thee bleeding
On the cross, to make us thine!
Now, our eyes for ever closing
To this fleeting world below,
On thy gentle breast reposing,
Teach us, Lord, thy grace to know.

2 Though unseen, be ever near us,
With the still small voice of love;

Whisp'ring words of peace to cheer us,
  Every doubt and fear remove :
Bring before us all the story
  Of thy life and death of woe ;
And, with hopes of endless glory,
  Wean our hearts from all below.

C.

"His right hand doth embrace me."—Song ii. 6.

1 How can I sink, with such a prop
  As the eternal God ;
Who bears the earth's huge pillars up
  And spreads the heavens abroad ?

2 How can I die while Jesus lives,
  Who rose and left the dead ?
Pardon and grace my soul receives
  From my exalted Head.

3 All that I am, all that I have,
  Shall be for ever thine ;
And all a duteous heart would give,
  My cheerful hands resign.

4 Yea, if I might make some reserve,
  And duty did not call ;

Thou lov'st me, Lord, with such a love,
That I would give Thee all.

CI.

"My beloved is mine, and I am His."—Song ii. 16.

1 SWEET Jesus! when I think on Thee,
My heart for joy doth leap in me:
Thy blest remembrance yields delight,
But far more sweet will be thy sight.

2 Of Him who did salvation bring,
I could for ever think and sing;
When with His name I'm charmed in song,
I wish myself all ear and tongue.

3 The joy's too great, I must confess;
I feel a bliss I can't express;
Thy love, my Saviour, ne'er can cloy,
Fountain of bliss, and source of joy!

4 O, let me ever share thy grace,
Still taste thy love, and view thy face!
Still let my tongue resound thy name,
And Jesus be my constant theme.

5 Bless'd Jesus, what delicious fare!
How sweet thy entertainments are!
Never did angels taste above
Redeeming grace and dying love!

CII.

"I found Him whom my soul loveth: I held Him and would not let Him go."—Song iii. 4.

1 O Holy Saviour, friend unseen,
  Since on thine arm thou bid'st us lean,
  Help us, throughout life's changing scene,
     By faith, to cling to Thee!

2 Far from our home, fatigu'd, opprest,
  Here we have found our place of rest,
  As exiles still, yet not unblest,
     While we can cling to Thee!

3 Without a murmur, we dismiss
  Our former dreams of earthly bliss;
  Our joy, our consolation, this—
     Each hour to cling to Thee!

4 What though the world deceitful prove,
  And earthly friends and hopes remove;

With patient uncomplaining love
  Still would we cling to Thee!

5 Oft when we seem to tread alone
  Some barren waste, with thorns o'ergrown,
  Thy voice of love, in gentlest tone,
    Whispers, " Still cling to Me!"

6 Though faith and hope may oft be tried,
  We ask not, need not aught beside,—
  So safe, so calm, so satisfied,
    The soul that clings to Thee!

CIII.

"Until the day break, and the shadows flee away, I will get me to the mountain of myrrh, and to the hill of frankincense."—Song iv. 6.

1 To watch the morning's dawn,
    I'll get me to the hill;
  And, till the shadows flee away,
    I'll keep the watch-tower still.

2 For morning surely comes,
    With everlasting light;
  The day star is at hand,
    To chase the dreary night.

3 Our journey has been long,
    And dark our desert-day :
The promis'd glory yet to come—
    Chief solace of our way.

4 And, though it lingers, yet
    It cheers the failing eye
To mark, amid surrounding gloom,
    The star of prophecy.

5 I'll trim my lamp the while,
    And chaunt a midnight lay,
Till perfect light and gladness come
    In glory's endless day.

CIV.

"Blow upon my garden, that the spices thereof may flow out."—Song iv. 16.

1 Love is the sweetest bud that blows :
    Its beauty never dies ;
On earth among the saints it grows,
    And ripens in the skies.

2 Oh, what a garden will be seen
    When all the flowers of grace

Appear in everlasting green
Before the Planter's face.

3 No more exposed to burning skies,
Or winter's piercing cold;
What never-dying sweets will rise
From every opening fold!

4 No want of sun or showers above
To make the flowers decline;
Fountains of life and beams of love
For ever spring and shine.

5 No more they need the quick'ning air,
Or gently rising dew,
Unspeakable their beauties are,
And yet for ever new.

6 Christ is their shade, and Christ their sun
Among them walks the King,
Whose presence is eternal noon—
Whose smile eternal spring.

CV.

"I sleep, but my heart waketh."—Song v. 2.

1 How sweet's the dream of her that sleeps,
    Even thee, thou happy Bride,
When choosing for thy rest the place
    Where thy Beloved died.

2 The bands that bound thy lover fast
    Unbind thee from thy pain;
His piercing cry, that soothes thy soul,
    And sings to sleep again.

3 The nails that fixed him to the cross
    Thy heavenly throne make sure;
He bears thee on His heart, thou Him,—
    Sleep on and rest secure.

4 Hush! stir not up the friend of Christ,
    Wake not the lovely Bride;
Some vision causeth her to smile:—
    She sees His open side!

CVI.

"I would cause her to drink of spiced wine of the juice of my pomegranate."—Song viii. 2.

1 Man of sorrows, and acquainted
    With our griefs, what shall we say?
Never language yet hath painted
    All the woes that on Thee lay.
Had I seen Thee cloth'd in weakness,
Bearing our reproach and sickness,
    To attend Thee day and night
    Would have been my heart's delight.

2 O that to this Heav'nly Stranger
    I had here my homage paid,
From His first sigh in the manger
    Till He cried " Tis finished !"
That first sigh had consecrated
Me His own, and I had waited
    On Him from His infancy,
    Serving Him unweariedly.

3 Walking, speaking, in devotion,
    Far to fields or forests stray'd,
I had watched every motion,
    And my Lord my pattern made.

More have angels ne'er desir'd
Than on Him,—or far retired,
  Or at home, awake, asleep—
  Fixed their wondering eyes to keep.

4 Tell me, little flock beloved,
  Ye on whom shone Jesus' face,
What within your souls then moved
  When ye felt His kind embrace?
O, disciple once most blessed,
As a bosom-friend caressed,
  Say, could e'er into thy mind
  Other objects entrance find?

5 Oft to prayer by night retreated,
  See Him from all search withdrawn,
Tearful eyes, and sighs repeated,
  Witness'd still the morning dawn.
There, where He made intercession,
I had pour'd forth my confession,
  And where for my sins He wept,
  Praying, I the watch had kept.

6 Should I thus to Thee have cleaved,
  Midst Thy poverty and woes,
On Thee, as my Lord believed,
  Or, perhaps, have joined thy foes?

Ah! Thy mercy I had spurn'd,
But Thyself my heart has turn'd.
Now Thou know'st, beneath, above,
Nought compared with Thee I love.

CVII.

"Set me as a seal upon thine heart, as a seal upon thine arm, for love is strong as death."—Song viii. 6.

1 BELOVED Saviour! let not me
In Thy kind heart forgotten be!
Of all that deck the field or bower,
Thou art the sweetest, fairest flower!

2 Youth's morn has fled, old age comes on,
But sin distracts my soul alone;
Beloved Saviour, let not me
In thy kind heart forgotten be!

CVIII.

"Make haste, my beloved."—Song viii. 14.

1 PASS away earthly joy,
  Jesus is mine!

Break every mortal tie,
　　　Jesus is mine!
Dark is the wilderness;
Distant the resting-place;
Jesus alone can bless:—
　　　Jesus is mine!

2 Tempt not my soul away,
　　　Jesus is mine!
Here would I ever stay,
　　　Jesus is mine!
Perishing things of clay,
Born but for one brief day,
Pass from my heart away,
　　　Jesus is mine!

3 Fare ye well, dreams of night,
　　　Jesus is mine!
Mine is a dawning bright,
　　　Jesus is mine!
All that my soul has tried
Left but a dismal void,
Jesus has satisfied,
　　　Jesus is mine!

4 Farewell mortality,
　　　Jesus is mine!

Welcome eternity,
    Jesus is mine!
Welcome ye scenes of rest,
Welcome ye mansions blest,
Welcome a Saviour's breast,
    Jesus is mine!

CIX.

"O Lord, I will praise Thee: though Thou wast angry with me, thine anger is turned away, and Thou comfortedst me."—Isa. xii. 1.

1 I will praise Thee every day,
Now thine anger's turn'd away!
Comfortable thoughts arise
From the bleeding sacrifice.

2 Here, in the fair gospel-field,
Wells of free salvation yield
Streams of life, a plenteous store,
And my soul shall thirst no more.

3 Jesus is become, at length,
My salvation and my strength!
And His praises shall prolong,
While I live, my pleasant song

4 Praise ye, then, His glorious name,
  Publish His exalted fame!
  Still His worth your praise exceeds,—
  Excellent are all His deeds.

5 Raise again the joyful sound,
  Let the nations roll it round!
  Zion shout, for this is He,
  God the Saviour dwells in thee.

CX.

"The Lord Jehovah is my strength and my song."
—Isa. xii. 2.

1 I'LL praise thee with my heart and tongue,
  O Lord, my soul's delight;
  Declaring to the world, in song,
  Thy glory, praise, and might.

2 Who spreads the lofty firmament,
  And starry skies around?
  Who makes the dew and rain descend
  To fructify the ground?

3 Who doth preserve our life and health,
  Our ease and safe abode?

Who doth secure our peace and wealth?
Our ever gracious God.

4 On Thee, Almighty Lord of Hosts,
Depends our life and all;
Thou keepest watch around our coasts,
Protectest great and small.

5 Thy chastisements are nought but love;
When we our sins confess,
We thy forgiveness richly prove;
'Tis thy delight to bless.

6 Thou count'st thy children's sighs and tears,
And know'st well why they mourn;
No tear too mean to Thee appears
To put into Thy urn.

7 Then murmur not, but be resign'd
To His most holy will;
Peace, rest, and comfort thou wilt find,
My soul, in being still.

CXI.

"Watchman! what of the night?"—Isa. xxi. 11.

1 WATCHMAN! tell us of the night,
  What its signs of promise are?
Traveller! o'er yon mountain's height,
  See that glory-beaming star!
Watchman! does its beauteous ray
  Aught of hope or joy foretell?
Traveller! yes: it brings the day—
  Promised day of Israel!

2 Watchman! tell us of the night;
  Higher yet that star ascends;
Traveller! blessedness and light,
  Peace and truth, its course portends.
Watchman! will its beams alone
  Gild the spot that gave them birth?
Traveller! ages are its own,
  And it bursts o'er all the earth.

3 Watchman! tell us of the night,
  For the morning seems to dawn:
Traveller! darkness takes its flight,
  Doubt and terror are withdrawn.

Watchman! let thy wanderings cease:
Hie thee to thy quiet home:
Traveller! lo! the Prince of Peace,
Lo! the Son of God is come!

CXII.

"In that day shall this song be sung in the land of Judah, We have a strong city; salvation will God appoint for walls and bulwarks."— Isa. xxvi. 1.

1 GLORIOUS things of thee are spoken,
    Zion, city of our God!
He, whose word cannot be broken,
    Form'd thee for His own abode:
On the Rock of Ages founded,
    What can shake thy sure repose?
With salvation's walls surrounded,
    Thou may'st smile at all thy foes.

2 See the streams of living waters,
    Springing from eternal love,
Well supply thy sons and daughters,
    And all fear of want remove:

Who can faint while such a river
  Ever flows their thirst t'assuage?
Grace, which like the Lord, the Giver,
  Never fails from age to age.

3 Round each habitation hov'ring,
  See the cloud and fire appear!
For a glory and a covering,
  Showing that the Lord is near:
Thus deriving from their banner
  Light by night and shade by day;
Safe they feed upon the manna
  Which He gives them when they pray.

4 Blest inhabitants of Zion,
  Wash'd in the Redeemer's blood!
Jesus, whom their souls rely on,
  Makes them kings and priests to God:
'Tis His love His people raises
  Over self to reign as kings,
And, as priests, His solemn praises
  Each for a thank-offering brings.

5 Saviour, if of Zion's city
  I, through grace, a member am;
Let the world deride or pity,
  I will glory in Thy name:

Fading is the worldling's pleasure,
　All his boasted pomp and show;
Solid joys and lasting treasure
　None but Zion's children know.

CXIII.

"Thine eyes shall see the King in His beauty they shall behold the land that is very far off."—Isa. xxxiii. 17.

1 O, what a lonely path were ours,
　　Could we, O Father, see
　No home of rest beyond it all,
　　No guide or help in Thee.

2 But thou art near, and with us still,
　　To keep us on the way
　That leads along this vale of tears
　　To the bright world of day.

3 There shall thy glory, O our God!
　　Break fully on our view:
　And we, thy saints, rejoice to find
　　That all thy word was true.

4 There Jesus, on His heav'nly throne
    Our wond'ring eyes shall see:
While we, the blest associates there
    Of all His joy shall be.

5 Sweet hope! we leave without a sigh
    A blighted world like this;
To bear the cross, despise the shame,
    For all that weight of bliss.

6 Yet little do thy saints, at best,
    Endure, O Lord, for Thee,
Whose suffering soul bore all our sins
    And sorrows on the tree:

7 Who faced our fierce and ruthless foe,
    Unaided and alone:
To win us for thy crown of joy,
    To raise us to Thy throne.

CXIV.

"He shall feed His flock like a shepherd."—
Isa. xl. 11.

1 Shepherd of thy little flock,
    Lead me to the shadowing rock;

Where the richest pasture grows,
Where the living water flows

2 By that pure and silent stream,
Shelter'd from the scorching beam;
Shepherd, Saviour, Guardian, Guide,
Keep me ever near Thy side.

CXV.

"He shall gather the lambs with His arm."—
Isa. xl. 11.

1 Jesus, tender Shepherd, hear me!
Bless thy little lamb to-night!
Through the darkness be Thou near me,
Watch my sleep till morning light!

2 All this day Thy hand has led me,
And I thank Thee for thy care;
Thou hast clothed me, warmed and fed me,
Listen to my evening prayer!

3 Let my sins be all forgiven!
Bless the friends I love so well!
Take me, when I die, to Heaven,
Happy there with thee to dwell!

CXVI.

"I will lead them in paths they have not known."
—Is. xlii. 16.

1 Lead, Saviour, lead, amid the encircling gloom
  Lead thou me on :
The night is dark, and I am far from home,
  Lead thou me on.
Keep thou my feet, I do not ask to see
The distant scene—one step enough for me.

2 I was not ever thus, nor pray'd that thou
  Should'st lead me on;
I lov'd to choose and see my path, but now
  Lead thou me on.
I lov'd the glare of day, and, spite of fears,
Pride rul'd my will; remember not past years.

3 So long Thy power hath bless'd me—sure it still
  Will lead me on,
O'er vale and hill, thro' stream and torrent, till
  The night is gone,
And, with the morn, those angel-faces smile
Which I have lov'd long since, and lost awhile.

CXVII.

"When thou passest through the waters, I will be with thee: and through the rivers they shall not overflow thee."—Isa. xliii. 2.

1 Be steady, be steady, O my soul!
   For the sea is come and the billows roll;
   With the help of God, and none beside,
   We shall safely pass the roaring tide.

2 Jesus-Jehovah be our stay
   Over the dark and troublous way;
   Embark'd in Him, we shall feel no fear,
   Though the storm, the trial of strength, be near.

3 Forget Him not! oh, my soul, remove
   All thoughts that breathe not of Jesus' love;
   His wondrous love, who freely gave
   His innocent life thy life to save.

4 Oh, let the sweet remembrance be
   Laid up in thine inmost treasury;
   There it shall brighten more and more,
   The most precious pearl in that secret shore.

CXVIII.

"He wakeneth morning by morning: He wakeneth mine ear to hear."—Isa. l. 4.

1 THE morning, the bright and the beautiful mornning
   Is up, and the sunshine is all on the wing,
With its fresh flush of gladness the landscape adorning,—
   A gladness which nothing but morning can bring.
The earth is awaking, the sky and the ocean,
   The river and forest, the mountain and plain;
The city is stirring its living commotion,
   And the pulse of the world is reviving again!

2 And we, too, awake, for our heavenly Father,
   Who soothed us so gently to sleep on His breast,
And made the soft stillness of evening to gather
   Around us, now calls us again from our rest.
But, ere to our labours and duties returning,
   We hasten to give Him the praise that is meet,
And, in solemn devotion, the first hours of morning,
   Our freest and freshest, we lay at His feet.

3 Then, happy in heart, not a moment delaying,
   In the breeze of the dawning, so pleasant and
      cool,
No loitering, no lingering, no trifling, no playing,
   But eager and active, we haste to the school.
How sweet are its hours, that shine o'er us so
      brightly !
   How pleasant its lessons, how short seems the
      day !
Its hours are but moments, they fly off so lightly,
   When we are so busy, so cheerful, and gay.

4 Then away to the school in the sweet summer
      morning,
   God's blessing upon us, his light on our road !
And let all the lessons we daily are learning,
   Be only to bring us more surely to God !
O now, let us haste to our heavenly Father,
   And, ere the fair skies of life's dawning be dim,
Let us come with glad hearts, let us come all together,
   And the morn of our youth let us hallow to Him.

CXIX.

"How beautiful upon the mountains are the feet of him that bringeth good tidings."—Isa. lii. 7.

1 Fair are the feet which bring the news
    Of gladness unto me;
What happy messengers are these
    Which my bless'd eyes do see?

2 These are the stars which God appoints
    For guides unto my way;
To lead my feet to Bethlehem,
    Where my dear Saviour lay.

3 These are my God's ambassadors,
    By whom His mind I know;
God's angels in his lower heaven,—
    God's trumpeters below.

4 The trumpet sounds, the dead arise
    Who fell by Adam's hand:
Again the trumpet sounds, and they
    Set forth for Canaan's land.

5 Thy servants speak—but thou, Lord, dost
    The hearing ear bestow;

They smite the rock—but Thou, my God,
    Dost make the waters flow.

6 Lord, thou, by them, dost guide my steps,
    That I may never stray;
The cloud and pillar march before,
    To show me Canaan's way.

7 I bless my God, who is my Guide;
    I sing in Zion's ways;—
When shall I sing on Zion's hill
    Thine everlasting praise?

CXX.

"His visage was so marred more than any man."
—Is. lii. 14.

1 O HEAD, so full of bruises,
    So full of pain and scorn;
'Mid other sore abuses,
    Mock'd with a crown of thorn!

2 O head, ere now surrounded
    With brightest majesty,
In death now bow'd and wounded,
    Accept this praise from me.

3 Thou countenance transcendant,
   From whom all glory shone,
To worlds, on Thee dependent;
   Now marred and spit upon.

4 What thee, O Lord, distracted,
   Was my soul's sinful load,
I had the debt contracted
   Which Thou did'st pay in blood.

CXXI.

"Who hath believed our report?"—Is. liii. 1.

1 Who hath our report believed?
   Shiloh come, is not received,
     Not received by His own.
Promis'd branch from root of Jesse,
David's offspring sent to bless you,
     Comes too lowly to be known.

2 Tell me, O thou favour'd nation,
   What is thy fond expectation,—
     Some fair spreading, lofty tree?
Let not worldly pride confound thee;
'Mong the lowly plants around thee,
     Mark the lowest—that is He.

3 Like a tender plant, that's growing
   Where no water's friendly flowing,
     No kind rains refresh the ground—
   Drooping, dying, ye shall view him,
   See no charms to draw you to him;
     There no beauty will be found.

4 Lo! Messiah, unrespected,
   Man of griefs—despis'd, rejected,
     Wounds His form disfiguring;
   Marr'd his visage more than any;
   For He bears the sins of many,
     All our sorrows carrying.

5 No deceit His mouth had spoken,
   Blameless, He no law had broken,
     Yet was numbered with the worst:
   For, because the Lord would grieve Him
   Ye who saw it did believe Him
     For his own offences curst.

6 But, while Him your thoughts accused,
   He for us alone was bruised;
     Yea, for us the victim bled!
   With His stripes our wounds are cured,
   By His pains our peace secured,
     Purchas'd with the blood He shed.

7 Love amazing, so to mind us!
  Shepherd come from Heaven to find us,
    Silly sheep, all gone astray;
  Lost, undone by our transgressions,
  Worse than stript of all possessions,
    Debtors without hope to pay.

8 Death our portion; slaves in spirit;
  He redeem'd us, by His merit,
    To a glorious liberty.
  Dearly first His goodness bought us,
  Truth and love then sweetly taught us,
    Truth and love have made us free.

9 Glory be to Him who gave us—
  Freely gave his Son to save us;
    Glory to the Son who came:
  Honour, blessing, adoration,
  Ever, from the whole creation,
    Be to God, and to the Lamb.

CXXII.

"He was wounded for our transgressions, He was bruised for our iniquities."—Is. liii. 5.

1 I lay my sins on Jesus,
    The spotless Lamb of God;
He bears them all, and frees us
    From the accursed load.
I bring my guilt to Jesus,
    To wash my crimson stains
White in His blood most precious,
    Till not a spot remains.

2 I lay my wants on Jesus:
    All fulness dwells in Him.
He heals all my diseases,
    He doth my soul redeem.
I lay my griefs on Jesus,
    My burdens and my cares;
He from them all releases,—
    He all my sorrows shares.

3 I rest my soul on Jesus,—
    This weary soul of mine;
His right hand me embraces,
    I on His breast recline.

I love the name of Jesus,
  Immanuel, Christ, the Lord;
Like fragrance on the breezes,
  His name abroad is poured.

4 I long to be like Jesus—
  Meek, loving, lowly, mild;
I long to be like Jesus,
  The Father's holy child;
I long to be with Jesus,
  Amid the Heavenly throng,
To sing, with saints, His praises,
  To learn the angels' song.

CXXIII.

"With His stripes we are healed."—Is. liii. 5.

1 O GRACE divine! the Saviour shed
  His life-blood on the cursed tree,
Bowed on the cross His blessed head,
  And died to make His brethren free.

2 Thro' suffering there, beneath His feet
  He trod the fierce avenger down:
There power itself and weakness meet—
  Emblem of each, yon thorny crown.

3 Fruit of the curse, the tangled thorn
   Showed that He bore its deadly sting;
  The crown, 'mid Israel's cruel scorn,
   Mark'd Him as earth's anointed King.

4 O blessed hour! when all the earth
   Its rightful Heir shall yet receive;
  When every tongue shall own His worth,
   And all creation cease to grieve.

5 Thou, dearest Saviour! Thou alone
   Can'st give thy weary people rest;
  And, Lord, till Thou art on the throne,
   This groaning earth can ne'er be blest.

CXXIV.

"Thy Maker is thy Husband."—Is. liv. 5.

1 WHAT earthly thing can thee annoy?
   HE made the earth to be:
  The waters cannot thee destroy,
   Thy Husband made the sea.

2 Fear'st thou the flaming element
   Will hurt, with burning ire?

Or that the scorching heat torment?—
Thy Husband made the fire.

3 No hurtful vapours shall destroy
　While He is pleased to spare ;
Thou shalt thy vital breath enjoy—
　Thy Husband made the air.

4 The sun that guides the golden day,
　The moon that rules the night,
The starry frame, the milky way,
　Thy Husband made for light.

5 The grazing herd, the beasts of prey,
　The creatures, great and small,
For thy behoof their tribute pay—
　Thy Husband made them all.

CXXV.

"The Gentiles shall come to thy light."—Is. lx. 3.

1 O'er the gloomy hills of darkness,
　Look, my soul, be still and gaze ;
All the promises do travail
　With a glorious day of grace.

Blessed jubilee!
Let thy glorious morning dawn.

2 Let the Indian, let the Negro,
Let the rude Barbarian see
That divine and glorious conquest,
Once obtain'd on Calvary;
Let the Gospel
Loud resound from pole to pole.

3 Kingdoms wide that sit in darkness,
Grant them, Lord, the glorious light;
And, from eastern coast to western,
May the morning chase the night,
And redemption,
Freely purchas'd, win the day.

4 Fly abroad, thou mighty Gospel,
Win and conquer, never cease;
May thy lasting wide dominions
Multiply and still increase;
Sway Thy sceptre,
Saviour, all the world around.

CXXVI.

"The Gentiles shall come to thy light, and kings to the brightness of thy rising."—Is. lx. 3.

1 O Zion, when thy Saviour came,
    In grace and love to thee,
No beauty in thy royal Lord
    Thy faithless eye could see.

2 Yet, onward in His path of grace
    The holy Suff'rer went,
To feel at last that love on thee
    Had all in vain been spent.

3 Yet not in vain—o'er Israel's land
    The glory yet will shine;
And He, thy once rejected King,
    For ever shall be thine.

4 Then thou, beneath the peaceful reign
    Of Jesus and His bride,
Shalt sound his grace and glory forth
    To all the earth beside.

5 The nations to thy glorious light,
    O Zion! yet shall throng;

And all the listening islands wait,
To catch the joyful song.

6 The name of Jesus yet shall ring
Through earth and heaven above:
And all His ransom'd people know
The Sabbath of His love.

CXXVII.

"All they from Sheba shall come: they shall bring gold and incense."—Is. lx. 6.

1 From Greenland's icy mountains,
From India's coral strand,
Where Afric's sunny fountains
Roll down their golden sand;
From many an ancient river,
From many a palmy plain,
They call us to deliver
Their land from error's chain.

2 What, though the spicy breezes
Blow soft on Ceylon's isle,—
Though every prospect pleases,
And only man is vile?

In vain, with lavish kindness,
    The gifts of God are strewn ;
The heathen, in his blindness,
    Bows down to wood and stone.

3 Shall we, whose souls are lighted
    With wisdom from on high —
Shall we to man benighted,
    The lamp of life deny ?
Salvation ! Oh, salvation !
    The joyful sound proclaim,
Till each remotest nation
    Has learnt Messiah's name.

4 Waft, waft, ye winds, His story,
    And you, ye waters, roll,
Till, like a sea of glory,
    It spreads from pole to pole :
Till o'er our ransom'd nature
    The Lamb, for sinners slain,
Redeemer, King, Creator,
    In bliss returns to reign.

CXXVIII.

"The Lord shall be thine everlasting light, and the days of thy mourning shall be ended."— Is. lx. 20.

1 HEAR what God the Lord hath spoken:
"O, my people, faint and few;
Comfortless, afflicted, broken,—
Fair abodes I build for you:
Thorns of heartfelt tribulation
Shall no more perplex your ways;
You shall name your walls Salvation,
And your gates shall all be praise.

2 "There, like streams that feed the garden,
Pleasures without end shall flow;
For the Lord, your faith rewarding,
All His bounty shall bestow:
Still, in undisturb'd possession,
Peace and righteousness shall reign;
Never shall you feel oppression,—
Hear the voice of war again.

3 "Ye, no more your suns descending,
Waning moons, no more shall see;

But your griefs, for ever ending,
    Find eternal noon in me :
God shall rise, and shining o'er you,
    Change to-day the gloom of night;
He, the Lord, shall be your glory—
    God, your everlasting light."

CXXIX.

" They are the seed which the Lord hath blessed."
—Is. lxi. 9.

1 I am a little child you see,
    My strength is little too,
But yet I fain would saved be ;
    Lord, teach me what to do.

2 My Saviour, hear ; Thou, for my good,
    Wert pleas'd a child to be ;
And Thou didst shed Thy precious blood
    Upon the cross for me.

3 My dearest Saviour, tell me how
    My thankfulness to show,
For all Thy love, before and now,
    Else I shall never know.

4 I think, since I so often hear
    That Thou dost want my heart,
  As Thy reward and purchase dear,
    That Thou in earnest art.

5 Come, then, and take this heart of mine—
    Come, take me as I am:
  I know that I by right am thine,
    Thou loving, gracious Lamb.

6 Down at thy feet still may I bow,
    Be thine, my Saviour, still;
  In nothing bad myself allow,
    Nor ever show self-will.

7 But I am weak, and nothing can
    Without thy Spirit do;
  Help me, O thou Almighty One,
    Help my companions too.

8 Preserve our little hearts secure
    From ev'ry hurt and stain;
  First make them, and then keep them pure
    And shut to all that's vain.

9 If early Thou wouldst take me hence,
    O, that no harm would be;

Into Thy arms I'll go at once
And ever live with Thee.

10 If thou wouldst have me longer stay,
In years and stature grow;
Help me to serve Thee night and day
While I am here below.

11 Then, after walking in Thy ways,
And serving Thee in love,
Put a blest end to these my days,
And take me hence above.

CXXX.

"I will mention the loving-kindnesses of the Lord, and the praises of the Lord, according to all that the Lord hath bestowed on us."—Is. lxiii. 7.

1 WE sing to God, whose tender love
Caused Him to leave His Throne above,
To dwell with sinful worms below,
And save them from eternal woe.

2 On fallen men He cast His eye,
In depths of mis'ry saw them lie,
Pitied their state, resolv'd to come,
And suffer freely in their room.

3 Our flesh He took, and died; then laid
Within an earthly tomb His head;
Then rose and took His seat on high,—
Ere long to come in majesty.

4 To Jesus, our exalted Head,
Immortal honours now be paid;
The glory of His saving name
Our tongues shall evermore proclaim.

CXXXI.
ANOTHER OF THE SAME.

1 Awake, my soul, in joyful lays,
And sing thy Great Redeemer's praise;
He justly claims a song from thee;
His loving-kindness, O how free!

2 He saw me ruin'd in the fall,
Yet lov'd me notwithstanding all,
He sav'd me from my lost estate;
His loving-kindness, O how great!

3 Though num'rous hosts of mighty foes,
Though earth and hell my way oppose,
He safely leads my soul along;
His loving-kindness, O how strong!

4 When trouble, like a gloomy cloud,
   Has gather'd thick, and thunder'd loud,
   He near my soul has always stood;
   His loving-kindness, O how good!

5 Often I feel my sinful heart,
   Prone from my Saviour to depart;
   But though I have Him oft forgot,
   His loving-kindness changes not!

6 Soon shall I pass the gloomy vale,
   Soon all my mortal pow'rs must fail;
   O, may my last expiring breath
   His loving-kindness sing in death!

7 Then let me mount and soar away
   To the bright world of endless day,
   And sing, with rapture and surprise,
   His loving-kindness in the skies!

CXXXII.

"Before they call I will answer."—Is. lxv. 24.

1 "O God!" was all night long the cry
   Of one oppressed with care,
  Till softened was his heart, and sweet
   Became his lips with prayer.

2 Then near the subtle tempter stole,
   And spake—" Fond babbler, cease,
   For not one *here am I* has God
   Ere sent to give you peace."

3 With sorrow sunk the suppliant's heart,
   And all his senses fled,
   When, lo! a messenger from God
   Thus gently spake, and said :—

4 " What ails thee now, my child, and why
   Art thou afraid to pray?
   And why thy former love dost thou
   Repent? Declare, and say."

5 " Ah," cries he, " never once to me
   Spake God, *here am I, son*,
   Cut off, methinks I am, and warned
   Far from His gracious throne."

6 To whom the messenger. " My son,
   The word from God I bear ;
   Go tell," he said, " yon mourner sunk
   In sorrow and despair,—

7 " Each *Lord appear* thy lips pronounce
   Contains my *here am I*,

A special messenger I send
Beneath thine every sigh.

8 "Thy love is but a girdle
Of the love I bear to thee,
And sleeping in thy *come, O Lord,*
There lies *here, son,* from me."

CXXXIII.

"Oh, that I had in the wilderness a lodging-place of wayfaring men; that I might leave my people, and go from them."—Jer. ix. 2.

1 Far from the world, O Lord, I flee,
From strife and tumult far;
From scenes where Satan wages still
His most successful war.

2 The calm retreat, the silent shade,
With prayer and praise agree;
And seem by Thy sweet bounty made
For those who follow Thee.

3 There, if Thy Spirit touch the soul,
And grace her mean abode;
Oh, with what peace, and joy, and love,
She communes with her God!

4 There, like the nightingale, she pours
　Her solitary lays;
　Nor asks a witness of her song,
　Nor thirsts for human praise.

5 Author and Guardian of my life,
　Sweet Source of light divine,
　And, (all harmonious names in one,)
　My Saviour, Thou art mine.

6 What thanks I owe Thee, and what love—
　A boundless, endless store—
　Shall echo through the realms above
　When time shall be no more.

CXXXIV.

"Weep ye not for the dead, neither bemoan him."
　—Jer. xxii. 10.

1 How blest the righteous when he dies!
　When sinks a weary soul to rest,
　How mildly beam the closing eyes;
　How gently heaves the expiring breast!

2 So fades a summer cloud away;
　So sinks the gale when storms are o'er;

So gently shuts the eye of day;
So dies a wave along the shore.

3 A holy quiet reigns around,
   A calm which life nor death destroys;
Nothing disturbs that peace profound
   Which his unfetter'd soul enjoys.

4 Farewell, conflicting hopes and fears,
   Where lights and shades alternate dwell!
How bright the unchanging morn appears:
   Farewell, inconstant world, farewell!

5 Life's duty done, as sinks the clay,
   Light from its load the spirit flies;
While heaven and earth combine to say,
   "How blest the righteous when he dies!"

CXXXV.

"The Lord our Righteousness."—Jer. xxiii. 6.

1 I once was a stranger to grace and to God;
  I knew not my danger, and felt not my load.
  Though friends spoke in rapture of Christ on the tree,
  Jehovah Tsidkĕnu was nothing to me.

2 I oft read with pleasure, to soothe or engage,
Isaiah's wild measure, and John's simple page;
But ev'n when they pictured the blood-sprinkled tree,
Jehovah Tsidkēnu seemed nothing to me.

3 Like tears from the daughters of Zion that roll,
I wept when the waters went over His soul:
Yet thought not that *my* sins had nailed to the tree
Jehovah-Tsidkēnu—'twas nothing to me.

4 When free grace awoke me by light from on high,
Then legal fears shook me, I trembled to die;
No refuge, no safety in self could I see—
Jehovah Tsidkēnu my Saviour must be.

5 My terrors all vanished before the sweet name;
My guilty fears banished, with boldness I came
To drink at the fountain, life-giving and free—
Jehovah Tsidkēnu is all things to me.

6 Jehovah Tsidkēnu! my treasure and boast—
Jehovah Tsidkēnu! I ne'er can be lost.
In Thee I shall conquer, by flood and by field—
My cable, my anchor, my breastplate and shield!

7 Even treading the valley, the shadow of death,
This watchword shall rally my faltering breath;
For while from life's fever my God sets me free,
Jehovah Tsidkēnu my death-song shall be.

CXXXVI.

"Then washed I thee with water......I clothed thee also with broidered work."—Ezek. xvi. 9, 10.

1 Hopeless and outcast once we lay,
　　Worthy Thy hate and scorn,
　But love like Thine could find a way
　　To rescue and adorn.

2 Dear Saviour, from Thy bleeding veins
　　A living fountain flows,
　To wash Thy bride from all her stains,
　　And soothe her deepest woes.

3 Cleansed from her sins, renew'd by grace,
　　Thy royal throne above,
　Dear Saviour, is her destined place,
　　Her sweet abode Thy love.

4 Thine eye, in that unclouded day,
　　Shall, with supreme delight,

Thy fair and glorious bride survey,
Unblemish'd in Thy sight.

CXXXVII.

"Behold I, even I, will both search my sheep and seek them out."—Ezek. xxxiv. 11.

1 Come, wandering sheep, O come!
   I'll bind thee to my breast;
   I'll bear thee to thy home,
     And lay thee down to rest.
     O come then to my breast,
     This is a blessed home,
     Come, wandering sheep, O come!

2 I saw thee stray forlorn,
   And heard thee faintly cry,
   And on the tree of scorn
     For thee I deign'd to die;
     What greater proof could I
     Give than to seek the tomb?
     Come, wandering sheep, O come!

3 I shield thee from alarms,
   And wilt not thou be blest?

I bear thee in my arms—
Thou bear me in thy breast.
O, this is love, come rest;
This is a blissful doom,—
Come, wandering sheep, O come!

CXXXVIII.

"I will set up one Shepherd over them, and He shall feed them."—Ezek. xxxiv. 23.

1 O Gracious Shepherd! bind us
With cords of love to Thee,
And evermore remind us
How mercy set us free.
O may Thy Holy Spirit
Set this before our eyes,
That we Thy death and merit
Above all else may prize.

2 We are of Thy salvation
Assured, through Thy love:
Yet O, on each occasion,
How faithless do we prove!
Thou hast our sins forgiven,—
Then, leaving all behind,

We would press on to Heaven,
Bearing the prize in mind.

3 Grant us, henceforth, dear Saviour,
While in this vale of tears,
To look to thee, and never
Give way to anxious fears;
Thou, Lord, wilt not forsake us,
Though we are oft to blame;
O, let thy love then make us
Hold fast thy faith and name.

CXXXIX.

"The judgment was set, and the books were opened."—Dan. vii. 10.

1   Day of judgment, day of wonders!
Hark! the trumpet's awful sound,
Louder than a thousand thunders,
Shakes the vast creation round!
How the summons will the sinner's heart confound!

2   See the Judge our nature wearing,
Cloth'd in majesty divine!
You who long for His appearing,

Then shall say, "This God is mine!"
Gracious Saviour, own me in that day for thine!

3 At His call the dead awaken,
   Rise to life from earth and sea;
   All the pow'rs of nature, shaken
   By His looks, prepare to flee:
Careless sinner, what will then become of thee?

4 Horrors past imagination
   Will surprise your trembling heart,
When you hear your condemnation,—
   "Hence, accursed wretch, depart!
Thou with Satan and his angels have thy part."

CXL.

"Though I sit in darkness, the Lord shall be a light unto me."—Micah vii. 8.

1 Ah! my dear Lord, whose changeless love
   To me, nor earth nor hell can part;
   When shall my feet forget to rove?
   Ah, what shall fix this faithless heart?

2 Why do these cares my soul divide,
   If Thou indeed hast set me free?

Why am I thus, if Thou hast died,—
If thou hast died to ransom me?

3 Around me clouds of darkness roll,
In deepest night I still walk on;
Heavily moves my fainting soul,
My comfort and my God are gone.

4 Oft with Thy saints my voice I raise,
And seem to join the tasteless song:
Faintly ascends the imperfect praise,
Or dies upon my powerless tongue.

5 Cold, weary, languid, heartless, dead,
To Thy dread courts I oft repair;
By conscience dragg'd, or custom led,
I come; nor know that God is there!

6 Nor yet the earthly Adam dies,
But lives, and moves, and fights again;
Still the fierce gusts of passion rise,
And rebel nature strives to reign.

7 O love, Thy sovereign aid impart!
And guard the gifts thyself hast given:
My portion Thou, my treasure art,
And life, and happiness, and heaven.

8 Would ought with Thee my wishes share,
    Though dear as life the idol be,
The idol from my breast I'll bear,
    Resolv'd to seek my all from Thee.

9 Whate'er I fondly counted mine,
    To Thee, my Lord, I here restore:
Gladly I all for Thee resign;
    Give me Thyself, I ask no more.

CXLI.

"Who is a God like unto Thee, that pardoneth iniquity."—Micah vii. 18.

1 GREAT God of wonders, all thy ways
    Are worthy of Thyself—divine;
But the bright glories of Thy grace
    Beyond Thine other wonders shine.
      Who is a pardoning God like Thee?
      Or who has grace so rich and free?

2 Such deep trangressions to forgive,
    Such guilty daring worms to spare,—
This is Thy grand prerogative,
    And in this honour none shall share.

Is there a pardoning God like thee?
Or is there grace so rich and free?

3 Pardon—from an offended God!
Pardon—for sins of deepest dye!
Pardon—bestowed through Jesus' blood!
Pardon—that brings the rebel nigh.
Where is the pardoning God like Thee?
Or where the grace so rich and free?

4 Oh, may this glorious, matchless love—
This godlike miracle of grace,—
Teach mortal tongues, like those above,
To raise this song of lofty praise.
Who is a pardoning God like Thee?
Or who has grace so rich and free?

CXLII.

"Your fathers, where are they?"—Zech. i. 5.

1 THE ancient days were days of might,
In forms of greatness moulded,
And flowers of heaven grew on the earth,
Within the Church unfolded:
For grace fell fast as summer dew,
And saints to giants' stature grew.

2 But one by one the gifts are gone
　　That in the Church resided,
And gone the Spirit's living light
　　That on her walls abided,
When by our shrines he came to dwell,
In power and presence visible.

3 A blight hath past upon the Church,
　　Her summer hath departed;
The chill of age is on her sons—
　　The cold and fearful-hearted:
And sad, amid neglect and scorn,
Our mother sits and weeps forlorn.

4 Narrower and narrower still each year
　　The holy circle groweth,
And what the end of all shall be
　　Nor man nor angel knoweth:
And so we wait and watch in fear,
It may be that the Lord is near.

CXLIII.

"I will dwell in the midst of thee."—Zech. ii. 10.

1 Son of God; Thy people shield!
    Must we still thine absence mourn?
  Let thy promise be fulfill'd,
    Thou hast said, " I will return!"

2 Gracious Leader, now appear,
    Shine upon us with Thy light!
  Like the spring, when Thou art near,
    Days and suns are doubly bright.

3 As a mother counts the days,
    Till her absent son she see,
  Longs and watches, weeps and prays,
    So our spirits long for Thee.

4 Come and let us feel Thee nigh,
    Then Thy sheep shall feed in peace;
  Plenty bless us from on high,
    Evil from amongst us cease.

5 Thus each day for Thee we'll spend,
    While our callings we pursue;
  And the thoughts of such a friend
    Shall each night our joy renew.

6 Let thy light be ne'er withdrawn,
　　Golden days afford us long!
　Thus we pray at early dawn,
　　This shall be our ev'ning song.

CXLIV.

"Turn you to the stronghold, ye prisoners of hope."
　　　　—Zech. ix. 12.

1 Come to the ark—come to the ark,
　　To Jesus come away;
　The pestilence walks forth by night,
　　The arrow flies by day.

2 Come to the ark—the waters rise,
　　The seas their billows rear;
　While darkness gathers o'er the skies,
　　Behold a refuge near!

3 Come to the ark—all, all that weep
　　Beneath the sense of sin;
　Without, deep calleth unto deep,
　　But all is peace within.

4 Come to the ark—ere yet the flood
　　Your ling'ring steps oppose;

Come, for the door which open stood
Is now about to close.

CXLV

"In that day there shall be a fountain opened for sin and for uncleanness."—Zech. xiii. 1.

1 THERE is a fountain filled with blood,
    Drawn from Immanuel's veins;
And sinners plung'd beneath that flood,
    Lose all their guilty stains.

2 The dying thief rejoiced to see
    That fountain in his day;
And there have I, as vile as he,
    Wash'd all my sins away.

3 Dear dying Lamb, thy precious blood
    Shall never lose its pow'r,
Till all the ransom'd Church of God
    Be sav'd, to sin no more.

4 E'er since, by faith, I saw the stream
    Thy flowing wounds supply,
Redeeming love has been my theme,
    And shall be till I die.

5 Then, in a nobler, sweeter song,
    I'll sing Thy power to save;
When this poor lisping, stamm'ring tongue
    Lies silent in the grave.

6 Lord, I believe thou hast prepar'd
    (Unworthy though I be,)
For me a blood-bought free reward,
    A golden harp for me!

7 'Tis strung, and tun'd for endless years,
    And form'd by pow'r divine;
To sound in God the Father's ears,
    No other name but Thine.

CXLVI.

"The Lord shall be King over all the earth."—
—Zech. xiv. 9.

1 'Tis come, the glad Millenial morn,—
    The Son of David reigns!
Sing, sing, O earth! for thou art free,
    And Satan is in chains.

2 Rejoice, for thou shalt fear no more
    The ruthless tyrant's rod;

Nor lose again the gracious smile
  Of thine incarnate God.

3 But chiefly thou, O Solyma!
  Thou queen of cities sing;
With shouts of triumph welcome now
  Thy Morning Star—thy King.

4 He, gracious Saviour, faithful still
  To thee, His faithless dove;
Forgives thee all, and bids thee dwell
  Within His breast of love.

5 On Him the happy myriads there
  Unwearied love to gaze:
There He, amid His brethren, dwells,
  The leader of their praise.

6 O blessed Lord! we little dream'd
  Of such a morn as this;
Such rivers of unmingled joy,
  Such full unbounded bliss.

7 And O! how sweet the happy thought,
  That all we taste or see,
We owe it to the dying Lamb—
  We owe it all to Thee!

8 Yes, dearest Saviour, one with Thee,
    Sweet source of joy divine;
In Thee we live, with Thee we reign,
    And we are wholly Thine.

CXLVII.

"Narrow is the way which leadeth unto life."—
Matt. vii. 14.

1 There is a path that leads to God,—
    All others go astray,—
Narrow, but pleasant, is the road;
    And Christians love the way.

2 It leads straight thro' this world of sin;
    And dangers must be past;
But those who boldly walk therein
    Will come to Heav'n at last.

3 Oh! lest my feeble steps should slide
    Or wander from Thy way,
Lord, condescend to be my guide,
    And I shall never stray.

4 Thus I may safely venture through,
    Beneath my Shepherd's care;

And keep the gate of Heav'n in view,
Till I shall enter there.

CXLVIII.

"Be harmless as doves."—Matt. x. 16.

1 AND is the Gospel peace and love?
 So let our conversation be;
 The serpent blended with the dove—
 Wisdom and meek simplicity.

2 Whene'er the angry passions rise,
 And tempt our thoughts or tongues to strife,
 To Jesus let us lift our eyes—
 Bright pattern of the Christian life.

3 Oh, how benevolent and kind!
 How mild, how ready to forgive!
 Be this the temper of our mind,
 And these the rules by which we live.

4 Thy fair example may we trace,
 To teach us what we ought to be;
 Make us, by Thy transforming grace,
 Dear Saviour, daily more like Thee.

CXLIX.

"Come unto me all ye that labour and are heavy-laden, and I will give you rest."—Matt. xi. 28.

1 Come, ye sinners, poor and wretched,
   Weak and wounded, sick and sore;
Jesus ready stands to save you,
   Full of mercy, joined with power.
     He is able,
   He is willing; doubt no more.

2 Ho! ye needy, come and welcome,
   God's free bounty glorify;
True belief, and true repentance,
   Every grace that brings us nigh;
     Without money,
   Come to Jesus Christ, and buy.

3 Let not conscience make you linger,
   Nor of fitness fondly dream!
All the fitness he requireth
   Is to feel your need of Him.
     This He gives you,
   'Tis the Spirit's rising beam.

4 Come, ye weary, heavy-laden,
   Lost and ruin'd by the fall,
   If you tarry till you're better,
   You will never come at all.
      Not the righteous,
   Sinners Jesus came to call.

5 View him prostrate in the garden,
   On the ground your Saviour lies,
   On the bloody tree behold him;
   Hear him cry before he dies,
      "It is finish'd!"
   Sinners, will not this suffice?

6 Lo! th' incarnate God, ascended,
   Pleads the merit of his blood,
   Venture on him, venture wholly,
   Let no other trust intrude;
      None but Jesus,
   Can do helpless sinners good.

7 Saints and angels join'd in concert,
   Sing the praises of the Lamb;
   While the blissful seats of heaven
   Sweetly echo with his name—
      Hallelujah!
   Sinners here may sing the same.

CL.

"Take my yoke upon you and learn of me."—
Matt. xi. 29.

1 Come ye souls, by sin afflicted,
  Bow'd with fruitless sorrow down;
By the broken law convicted,
  Thro' the cross see pardon won.
    Look to Jesus!
  Mercy flows thro' him alone.

2 Take his easy yoke and wear it;
  Love will make obedience sweet,
Christ will give you strength to bear it,
  While his wisdom guides your feet
    Safe to glory,
  Where his ransom'd captives meet.

3 Sweet as home to pilgrims weary,
  Light to newly-opened eyes,
Or full springs in deserts dreary,
  Is the rest the cross supplies:
    All who taste it
  Shall to life immortal rise.

4 While the wounds of woe are healing,
   When the heart is all resigned,
   'Tis the solemn feast of feeling,
   'Tis the Sabbath of the mind.
     None but Jesus
   Can the broken heart unbind.

5 Blessed are the eyes that see him,
   Blest the ears that hear his voice;
   Blessed are the souls that trust him,
   And in him alone rejoice.
     His commandments
   Then become their happy choice.

6 But to sing the rest of glory,
   Mortal tongues far short must fall;
   Tongues celestial strive to reach it,
   But it soars beyond them all.
     Faith believes it—hope expects it—
     Love desires it—
   But it overwhelms them all!

CLI.

"Ye shall find rest unto your souls."—Matt. xi. 29.

1 Does the gospel-word proclaim
   Rest for those who weary be?

Then, my soul, put in thy claim,
  Sure that promise speaks to thee:
Marks of grace I cannot show,
  All polluted is my best;
Yet I weary am, I know,
  And the weary long for rest.

2 Burden'd with a load of sin,
    Harrass'd with tormenting doubt,
  Hourly conflicts from within,
    Hourly crosses from without;
  All my little strength is gone,
    Sink I must without supply;
  Sure upon the earth is none,
    Can more weary be than I.

3 In the ark the weary dove
    Found a welcome resting-place;
  Thus my spirit longs to prove
    Rest in Christ, the ark of grace;
  Tempest-toss'd I long have been,
    And the flood increases fast;
  Open, Lord, and take me in
    Till the storm be overpast.

4 Safely lodg'd within thy breast,
    What a wondrous change I find;

Now I know thy promis'd rest
  Can compose a troubled mind:
You that weary are like me,
  Hearken to the gospel-call;
To the ark for refuge flee,
  Jesus will receive you all!

CLII.

"My yoke is easy and my burden is light."—
Matt. xi. 30.

1 Light is the yoke that, lined with love,
    The willing neck confines;
  When ready feet obedient move,
    As He who rules inclines.

2 The burden's light that love lays on,
    By willing strength up-borne;
  When true the heart it rests upon,
    To a sweet service sworn.

3 On me thy yoke, my Saviour, lay,
    And make my spirit meek;
  That I may love to tread thy way,
    Nor other pathway seek.

4 When I on Thee my burden rest,
　　Thy burden, Lord, be mine;
　I of thy love, joy, peace possest,
　　My sin and guilt all thine.

CLIII.

"If any man will come after me, let him deny himself, and take up his cross and follow me."
—Matt. xvi. 24.

1 Come, my fond fluttering heart,
　　Come, struggle to be free;
　Thou and the world must part,
　　However hard it be:
　My trembling spirit owns it just,
　But cleaves yet closer to the dust.

2 Ye tempting sweets, forbear,
　　Ye dearest idols fall;
　My love ye must not share,
　　Jesus shall have it all:
　'Tis bitter pain, 'tis cruel smart,
　But ah! thou must consent, my heart!

3 Ye fair enchanting throng!
　　Ye golden dreams, farewell!

Earth has prevail'd too long,
And now I break the spell:
Ye cherish'd joys of early years—
Jesus, forgive these parting tears.

4 But must I part with all?
My heart still fondly pleads:
Yes, Dagon's self must fall,—
It beats, it throbs, it bleeds.
Is there no balm in Gilead found,
To soothe and heal the smarting wound?

5 O yes, there is a balm,
A kind physician there,
My fever'd mind to calm,
To bid me not despair;
Aid me, dear Saviour, set me free,
And I will all resign to Thee.

6 O may I feel Thy worth,
And let no idol dare,
No vanity of earth
With Thee, my Lord, compare:
Now bid all worldly joys depart,
And reign supremely in my heart!

CLIV.

"While the bridegroom tarried they all slumbered and slept."—Matt. xxv. 5.

1 When a careless world is sleeping,
　Then it is the day will come;
Mirth shall then be turn'd to weeping
　Sinners then shall meet their doom.
But the people of the Lord
Shall obtain their bright reward.

2 Waiting for our Lord's returning,
　Be it ours his word to keep;
Let our lamps be always burning,
　Let us watch while others sleep:
We're no longer of the night,
We are children of the light.

3 Being of the blessed number,
　Whom the Saviour calls his own,
'Tis not meet that we should slumber
　When the night is almost gone,
And from heaven is heard the cry
Which proclaims the Bridegroom nigh.

CLV.

"At midnight there was a cry made, Behold the Bridegroom cometh."—Matt. xxv. 6.

1 YE virgin souls, arise,
    With all the dead, awake;
Unto salvation wise,
    Oil in your vessels take;
Up-starting at the midnight cry,
Behold the heavenly Bridegroom nigh.

2 He comes, he comes to call
    The nations to His bar,
And raise to glory all
    Who fit for glory are.
Make ready for your full reward,
Go forth with joy to meet your Lord.

3 Go, meet Him in the sky,
    Your everlasting friend:
Your head to glorify
    With all his saints ascend;
Ye pure in heart obtain the grace
To see, without a veil, his face.

4 Ye, that have here received
    The unction from above;

And in His Spirit lived,
    Obedient to his love ;
Jesus shall claim you for His bride ;
Rejoice with all the sanctified.

5 Rejoice in glorious hope
    Of that great day unknown,
When you shall be caught up,
    To stand before his throne,
Called to partake the marriage feast,
And lean on our Immanuel's breast.

6 Then let us wait to hear
    The trumpet's welcome sound ;
To see our Lord appear,
    May we be watching found ;
Enrobed in righteousness divine,
In which the bride shall ever shine.

CLVI.

"Go ye out to meet him."—Matt. xxv. 6.

1 CHILDREN of light, awake ! awake !
    Ye slumbering virgins rise ;
Go, meet the Royal Bridegroom now
    And show that ye are wise.

2 Through love the Man of Sorrows oft
   Hath watched and wept for you;
   Then gave away his life to prove
   That all that love was true.

3 Then wake! for lo, the midnight cry
   Of warning in the air,
   Bids all his church to greet him now,
   Their dying lamps prepare.

CLVII.

"Take, eat, this is my body."—Matt. xxvi. 26.

1 BREAD of the world, in mercy broken!
   Wine of the soul, in mercy shed!
   By whom the words of life were spoken,
   And in whose death our sins are dead.

2 Look on the heart by sorrow broken;
   Look on the tears by sinners shed,
   And be thy feast to us the token,
   That by thy grace our souls are fed.

CLVIII.

"Lo, I am with you alway."—Matt. xxviii. 20.

1 Who but a Christian thro' all life
    The blessing may prolong?
Who thro' the world's sad day of strife
    Still chaunt his morning song?

2 Fathers may hate us or forsake,
    God's foundlings then are we;
Mother on child no pity take,
    But we shall still have Thee.

3 We may look home and seek in vain
    A fond paternal heart,
But Christ hath given his promise plain
    To do a brother's part.

4 Nor shall dull age, as worldlings say,
    The heavenward flame annoy;
The Saviour cannot pass away,
    And with Him lives our joy.

5 Such is our banquet, dearest Lord;
    O give us grace to cast
Our lot with thine, to trust thy word,
    And keep our best till last.

CLIX.

"Come, take up the Cross and follow me."—Mark x. 21.

1 Jesus, I my cross have taken,
  All to leave and follow Thee;
 Naked, poor, despised, forsaken,
  Thou from hence my all shalt be.
 Perish, every fond ambition,
  All I've sought, or hop'd, or known,
 Yet how rich is my condition,
  God and heaven are still my own.

2 Let the world despise and leave me,
  They have left my Saviour too;
 Human hearts and looks deceive me,
  Thou art not, like them, untrue.
 And whilst Thou shalt smile upon me,
  God of wisdom, love, and might,
 Foes may hate and friends disown me—
  Show thy face and all is bright.

3 Go, then, earthly fame and treasure,
  Come, disaster, scorn, and pain,
 In thy service pain is pleasure,
  With Thy favour loss is gain.

I have called Thee, Abba, Father,
　　I have set my heart on Thee;
Storms may howl, and clouds may gather,
　　All must work for good to me.

4 Man may trouble and distress me,
　　'Twill but drive me to thy breast;
Life with trials hard may press me,
　　Heaven will bring me sweeter rest.
O 'tis not in grief to harm me,
　　While thy love is left to me;
O, 'twere not in joy to charm me,
　　Were that joy unmixed with Thee.

5 Soul, then know thy full salvation,
　　Rise o'er sin, and fear, and care;
Joy to find in every station,
　　Something still to do or bear.
Think what spirit dwells within thee;
　　Think what Father's smiles are thine;
Think that Jesus died to win thee;
　　Child of heaven, can'st thou repine?

6 Haste thee on from grace to glory,
　　Armed by faith, and winged by prayer,
Heaven's eternal day's before thee,
　　God's own hand shall guide thee there.

Soon shall close thy earthly mission,
Soon shall pass thy pilgrim days,
Hope shall change to glad fruition,
Faith to sight, and prayer to praise.

CLX.

"There was darkness over the whole land until the ninth hour."—Mark xv. 33.

1 Lo, at noon 'tis sudden night!
   Darkness covers all the sky!
   Rocks are rending at the sight!
   Children, can you tell me why?
   What can all these wonders be?
   Jesus dies on Calvary!

2 Nail'd upon the cross, behold
   How his tender limbs are torn!
   For a royal crown of gold
   They have made him one of thorn.
   Cruel hands that dare to bind
   Thorns upon a brow so kind!

3 See! the blood is falling fast
   From his forehead and his side!

Hark! he now has breath'd his last!
With a mighty groan he died!
Children, shall I tell you why
Jesus condescends to die?

4 He who was a king above,
   Left his kingdom for a grave,
Out of pity and of love,
   That the guilty he might save!
Down to this sad world he flew,
For such little ones as you!

5 You were wretched, weak, and vile
   You deserv'd his holy frown;
But he saw you with a smile,
   And to save you hasten'd down,
Listen, children;—this is why
Jesus condescends to die.

CLXI.

"The Lord God shall give unto him the throne of his father, David."—Luke i. 32.

1 'Tis He! the mighty Saviour comes,
   The victory now is won!

And lo! the throne of David waits
For David's royal Son.

2 Thou blessed Heir of all the earth!
Ascend Thine ancient throne,
And bid the willing nations now
Thy peaceful sceptre own.

3 Shine forth in all Thy glory, Lord,
That man at length may see
That joy, so long estranged from earth,
Can only spring from Thee.

4 O happy day! 'tis come at last,
The reign of death is o'er;
And sin, that marr'd our sweetest joys
Shall grieve our hearts no more.

5 Wash'd in Thy blood, the tribes of earth,
With all the blest above,
Shall dwell in peace, united now,
One family of love.

6 Fruit of Thy toil, Thou bleeding Lamb!
These joys we owe to Thee,
Then take the glory, Lord!—'tis Thine!—
And shall for ever be.

CLXII.

"Unto you is born this day a Saviour."—Luke ii. 11.

1 Lo the eventful day, bestowed
   Upon a sinful world by God!
   To Him that made the worlds, this day
   O all ye worlds, your homage pay.

2 That life to sinners might be given,
   The great Creator comes from heaven;
   In flesh his glory veils, that He
   The Saviour of the lost may be.

3 Saviour! for us a child of days,
   Thee with our hearts and tongues we praise;
   Joyous to Thee we lift the song
   Once sung by Bethlehem's angel-throng.

4 Wondrous compassion! for our sake
   Thou didst of flesh and blood partake,
   Our friend, our elder brother, Thou,
   We God the Father's children now.

5 By one man's trespass lost were we,
   But one Redeemer makes us free;
   Behold, the chiefest child of wrath
   Believing, full salvation hath.

6 New glories, O ye heavens, accord
This day in honour of your Lord!
Rejoice, thou nether earth, and bring
New songs to celebrate your King.

7 Lo the eventful day bestowed
Upon a sinful world by God!
Well may the whole creation pay
Homage to Jesus on this day!

CLXIII.

"Ye shall find the babe lying in a manger."—
Luke ii. 12.

1 AWAKE my heart, my soul, my eyes;
See what in yonder manger lies!
Whose is that helpless, new-born child!
'Tis Christ by whom we're reconciled.

2 Welcome, thrice welcome, heavenly guest,
God in our flesh made manifest!
Descending from thy throne on high,
For us to live, for us to die.

3 If this one world did thousands hold,
Adorn'd with precious stones and gold:

Yet all these worlds on worlds would be
A cradle far too mean for Thee.

4 Yet, Lord, Thou wilt my dwelling share,
And for Thyself a couch prepare,
To rest for ever in my heart,
That I from Thee may never part!

CLXIV.

"Glory to God in the highest, and on earth peace."
Luke ii. 14.

1 Hark! the herald angels sing,
" Glory to the new-born King!
Peace on earth, and mercy mild,
God and sinners reconcil'd."

2 Joyful, all ye nations rise,
Join the triumph of the skies;
Hail the heav'n-born Prince of Peace,
Hail the Sun of Righteousness.

3 Mild he lays his glory by,
Born that man no more might die.
Born to raise the sons of earth,
Born to give them second birth.

4 " Glory to the new-born King!"
   Let us all the anthem sing;
   " Peace on earth, and mercy mild,
   God and sinners reconcil'd."

5 Joyful, all ye nations, rise,
   Join the triumph of the skies;
   With th' angelic host proclaim,
   " Christ is born in Bethlehem."

CLXV.
" Peace be to this house."—Luke x. 5.

1 PEACE be to this habitation;
   Peace to all that dwell therein;
   Peace, the earnest of salvation;
   Peace, the fruit of pardoned sin;
   Peace, that speaks the heavenly Giver;
   Peace to worldly minds unknown;
   Peace divine, that lasts for ever,
   Peace, that comes from God alone.

2 Prince of Peace, be present near us,
   Fix in all our hearts thy home;
   With thy gracious presence cheer us;
   Let thy sacred kingdom come;

Raise to heaven our expectation ;
Give our favoured souls to prove,
Glorious and complete salvation,
In the realms of bliss above.

CLXVI.

"Not my will, but Thine be done."—Luke xxii. 42.

1 My God, my Father, while I stray,
　Far from my home, on life's rough way,
　O teach me from my heart to say,
　　　　　"Thy will be done!"

2 If thou shouldst call me to resign,
　What most I prize—it ne'er was mine;
　I only yield Thee what is thine ;
　　　　　"Thy will be done."

3 Should pining sickness waste away
　My life in premature decay,
　My Father, still I strive to say,
　　　　　"Thy will be done!"

4 If but my fainting heart be blest
　With thy sweet spirit for its guest,
　My God, to Thee I leave the rest;—
　　　　　"Thy will be done!"

5 Renew my will from day to day;
Blend it with thine, and take away
All that now makes it hard to say
      "Thy will be done!"

6 Then when on earth, I breathe no more,
The prayer oft mix'd with tears before,
I'll sing when on a happier shore
      "Thy will be done!"

CLXVII.

"And Peter went out and wept bitterly."—Luke xxii. 62.

1 Flow fast, my tears, the cause is great;
  This tribute claims an injured friend:
One whom I long pursued with hate,
  And yet He loved me to the end.
When death his terrors round me spread,
And aimed his arrows at my head,
Christ interposed—the wound He bore,
And bade the monster dare no more.

2 Fast flow my tears, yet faster flow,
  Stream copious as yon purple tide,

'Twas I that dealt the deadly blow,
  I urged the hand that pierced his side.
Keen pangs and agonizing smart
Oppress his soul and rend his heart;
While justice, armed with power divine,
Pours on his head, what's due to mine.

3 Fast, and yet faster flow my tears,
  Love breaks the heart, and drowns the eyes;
His visage marr'd, towards heaven he rears,
  And pleading for his murderers, dies!
My grief nor measure knows no end,
Till He appears the sinner's friend!
And gives me in a happy hour,
To feel the risen Saviour's power.

CLXVIII.

"When they were come to a place called Calvary, there they crucified him."—Luke xxiii. 33.

1 THERE is a sacred, hallow'd spot,
    Oft present to mine eye;
  By saints it ne'er can be forgot,
    'Tis much lov'd Calvary.

2 Eventful mount! Oh, what a scene
    Of love and agony,

Was there display'd, when Christ was seen
Groaning on Calvary.

3 'Twas there he vanquish'd hell and death,
And with a conqueror's cry,
" 'Tis finish'd," he resigned his breath,
On much lov'd Calvary.

4 Endeared mount, for earthly joys,
Let others pass thee by ;
Earth's transient scenes, and fading toys,
I'll leave for Calvary.

5 When fainting under guilt's dread load,
Then to the cross I'll fly ;
And trust the merit of that blood,
Which flows from Calvary.

6 When'er I feel temptation's pow'r,
On Jesus I'll rely ;
And in the sharp conflicting hour,
Repair to Calvary.

7 And when around the feast of love,
Then will I fix mine eye,
On Him who intercedes above,
Who bled on Calvary.

8   When the dread scene of death, the last
      Important hour draws nigh;
    Then with my dying eyes I'll cast
      A look on Calvary.

CLXIX.

"He is not here, but is risen."—Luke xxiv. 6.

1 "The Lord is risen"—O what joy
      These blessed tidings give!
    He died our enemies to destroy,
      He lives, we therefore live.

2 "The Lord is risen"—death and sin,
      And hell all conquered are;
    He's gone the holiest within,
      Our mansion to prepare.

3 Our place is with Him on the throne,
      There, with the Lord we love;
    As strangers here ourselves we own,
      Our hearts, our home, above.

CLXX.

ANOTHER OF THE SAME.

1 THE happy morn is come;
Triumphant o'er the grave,
The Saviour leaves the tomb,
Almighty now to save.
 Captivity is captive led,
 Since Jesus liveth that was dead.

2 Who now accuseth them
For whom the surety died,
Or who shall those condemn
Whom God has justified?
 Captivity is captive led,
 Since Jesus liveth that was dead.

3 Christ hath the ransom paid,
The glorious work is done;
On Him our help is laid,
The victory is won.
 Captivity is captive led,
 Since Jesus liveth that was dead.

4 Hail the triumphant Lord,
The resurrrection thou!

Hail the incarnate Word,
 Before thy throne we bow.
  Captivity is captive led,
  Since Jesus liveth that was dead.

CLXXI.

"The Lord is risen indeed."—Luke xxiv. 34.

1 Christ, the Lord, is risen to-day!
 Sons of men and angels say;
 Raise your joys and triumphs high,
 Sing, ye heav'ns—and earth reply.

2 Love's redeeming work is done;
 Fought the fight, the battle won;
 Lo! the sun's eclipse is o'er;
 Lo! he sets in blood no more.

3 Vain the stone, the watch, the seal;
 Christ hath burst the gates of hell;
 Death in vain forbids his rise,
 Christ hath open'd Paradise.

4 Lives again our glorious King,
 "Where, O death! is now thy sting!"
 Once He died, our souls to save;
 "Where's thy vict'ry, boasting grave?"

5 Soar we now where Christ has led,
    Following our exalted head ;
    Made like him, like him we rise,
    Ours the cross, the grave, the skies.

CLXXII.

"All things were made by Him."—John. i. 3.

1 ALL glory to the eternal Word,
    Earth's Lord and King!
  All glory to the eternal Word,
    Ye angels sing.
    Ye sons of earth your tribute bring,
        His name
        Proclaim,—
    Jehovah—God—the Lord;
    Ever to be adored.
  Maker of all,
    Before Him prostrate fall.
  By every voice, and tribe, and tongue,
  For ever and for ever be his praises sung.

2 This green, glad, goodly earth of ours
    His hand did frame.

This green, glad, goodly earth of ours
  Doth still proclaim
By day and night his wondrous name.
    These seas
    Are His;
  Each mountain-peak that towers,
  These clouds with their fresh showers,
These streams that run,
Quick-glancing in the sun,
These tossing woods, these trembling flowers,
And all that men call bright in this bright world of ours.

3 All that has life and breath he made,
    In earth, sea, sky,
  All that has life and breath he made
    To swim or fly—
  To creep or bound; and in his eye,
    All good
    They stood,
    In beauty pure arrayed,
    As if they could not fade.
  How fair this frame,
  How excellent his name,
Who, in the fulness of his love,
Transplanted thus to earth the Paradise above!

CLXXIII.

"Of his fulness have all we received, and grace for grace."—John i. 16.

1 RICHES immense are in thy hand,
Thou God in whom I trust;
In whom I live, by whom I stand,
Most holy, wise, and just.

2 O how unbounded is thy grace,
How rich, how full, how free!
The needy thou delight'st to raise;
I'll tell my wants to Thee.

3 I want to fear thy sacred name,
I want to love Thee more;
I want to feel that heavenly flame
Which I have felt before.

4 I want to know myself aright,
To hear what Jesus saith;
I want repentance in thy sight,
I want a stronger faith.

5 I want to have my soul resigned
Submissive to thy will;

I want a meek, and humble mind ;
　　I want my wants to feel.

6 I want a chaste and single eye :
　　Thy gracious ear incline !
　From fulness infinite supply
　　This empty soul of mine.

7 Through Jesus let these blessings flow,
　　He bought them with his blood ;
　Now let a worthless sinner know
　　Thy promises made good.

CLXXIV.

"Whosoever drinketh of the water that I shall give him, shall never thirst."—John iv. 14.

1 Sweet was the hour, O Lord, to Thee,
　　At Sychar's lonely well,
　When a poor outcast heard Thee there
　　Thy great salvation tell.

2 Thither she came ; but, O, her heart,
　　All filled with earthly care,
　Dream'd not of Thee, nor thought to find
　　The hope of Israel there.

3 Lord! 'twas thy power unseen that drew
   The stray one to that place,
In solitude to learn from Thee
   The secrets of Thy grace.

4 There Jacob's erring daughter found
   Those streams unknown before,
The water-brooks of life that make
   The weary thirst no more.

5 And, Lord, to us, as vile as she,
   Thy gracious lips have told
That mystery of love, revealed
   At Jacob's well of old.

6 In spirit, Lord, we've sat with Thee
   Beside the springing well
Of life and peace—and heard Thee there
   Its healing virtues tell.

7 Dead to the world, we dream no more
   Of earthly pleasures now;
Our deep, divine, unfailing spring
   Of grace and glory, Thou.

CLXXV.

ANOTHER OF THE SAME.

1 Sweeter, O Lord, than rest to Thee,
  While seated by the well,
Was Thine own task of love, to all
  Of grace and peace to tell.

2 One thoughtless heart that never knew
  The pulse of life before,
There learn'd to love—was taught to sigh,
  For earthly joys no more.

3 Friend of the lost, O Lord, in Thee,
  Samaria's daughter there
Found One whom love had drawn to earth,
  Her weight of guilt to bear.

4 Fair witness of Thy saving grace,
  In her, O Lord, we see,
The wandering soul by love subdued,
  The sinner drawn to Thee.

5 Through all that sweet and blessed scene,
  Dear Saviour, by the well,
More than enough the trembler finds,
  His guilty fears to quell.

6 There, in the full repose of faith,
    The soul delights to see,
  Not only one who deeply loves,
    But *Love itself* in Thee.

CLXXVI.

"Him that cometh to me I will in no wise cast out."—John vi. 37.

1 Just as I am—without one plea
    But that thy blood was shed for me,
    And that thou bid'st me come to Thee,
      O Lamb of God, I come.

2 Just as I am—and waiting not
    To rid my soul of one dark spot—
    To Thee whose blood can cleanse each blot,
      O Lamb of God, I come.

3 Just as I am—tho' toss'd about
    With many a conflict, many a doubt,
    Fightings within and fears without,
      O Lamb of God, I come.

4 Just as I am—poor, wretched, blind,
    Sight, riches, healing of the mind,

Yea, all I need in Thee to find—
O Lamb of God, I come.

5 Just as I am—thou wilt receive,
Wilt welcome, pardon, cleanse, relieve,
Because thy promise I believe,
O Lamb of God, I come.

6 Just as I am—thy love I own
Has broken every barrier down;
Now to be thine, yea, thine alone—
O Lamb of God, I come.

CLXXVII.

"He calleth his own sheep by name, and leadeth them out."—John x. 3.

1 Jesus, lead us, by thy power
Safe into the promised rest;
Hide our souls within thine arms,
Let us lean upon thy breast.

2 Nothing can preserve our going,
But salvation full and free;
Nothing can our souls dishearten
But our absence, Lord, from thee.

3 In thy presence we are happy,
  In thy presence we're secure;
  In thy presence all afflictions
  We can easily endure.

4 In thy presence we can conquer,
  We can suffer, we can die;
  Far from Thee we faint and languish;
  O, our Saviour, keep us nigh.

CLXXVIII.

"No man is able to pluck them out of my Father's hand."—John x. 29.

1 Tho' twice ten thousand sinners go
  Down to the pit of endless woe,
  God's choice from all repentance free,
  The guard of his elect shall be.

2 To fall from that, if God be true,
  No sinner shall whom He foreknew;
  Whom God will save to God must rise,
  And fill a mansion in the skies.

3 Triumphant grace shall ever keep
  The weakest of the way-worn sheep;

Salvation's free and shall be given,
To all who trust the God of heaven.

CLXXIX.

ANOTHER OF THE SAME.

1 Saved from the awful guilt of sin,
   By Him who bare the cross ;
We'll now a cheerful strain begin,
   Where God began with us.

2 We sing the vast unmeasured grace,
   Of height and depth untold,
Which did the saints elect embrace
   As sheep within the fold.

3 We had not known the blood for sin,
   Nor sweets of pardoning love,
Unless our worthless name had been
   Enrolled for life above.

4 Well may we sing, since bought with blood
   Of God's eternal Son ;
O how secure God's purpose stood,
   Ere time its race begun !

CLXXX.

"If I wash thee not, thou hast no part with me."
—John xiii. 8.

1 For ever here my rest shall be,
    Close to thy bleeding side :
  This all my hope, and all my plea,
    For me the Saviour died.

2 My dying Saviour, and my God,
    Fountain for guilt and sin,
  Sprinkle me ever with thy blood,
    And cleanse and keep me clean.

3 Wash me, and make me thus thine own,
    Wash me, and mine thou art,
  Wash me, but not my feet alone,
    My hands, my head, my heart.

4 Th' atonement of thy blood apply,
    Till faith to sight improve ;
  Till hope in full fruition die,
    And all my soul be love.

CLXXXI.

*"In my Father's house are many mansions."—
John xiv. 2.*

1 Star-gemm'd floor of the land I love,
    Tell me, and tell me now,
What are the many glittering pearls
    Which hang on thy jewelled brow?

2 Schoolmen write in the lettered page,
    That each is a world like ours;
But where sky-birds sing superior songs,
    In more delightful bowers.

3 Where the wolf and the lamb in concord meet,
    Where the leopard harmless lives,
And where undewed with the sweat of man,
    The field its harvest gives.

4 Where sin hath shed no withering blight,
    Where death no entrance gains,
Where the men of a thousand years ago,
    Still bound across the plains.

5 Many, if such ye be, fair worlds,
    Would ask no brighter doom,

Than within your gorgeous palaces
To find a lasting home.

6 So let them, more ambitious, I
More towering wishes frame—
I would not dwell in these but with
The Lord of all of them.

7 They may be near to the pearly gates,
They may stand close to heaven,
But who would live in the servant's lodge
If the mansion-house were given?

CLXXXII.

"I am the way."—John xiv. 6.

1 JESUS, my all, to heaven is gone,
He whom I fix my hopes upon!
His track I see, and I'll pursue
The narrow way, till Him I view.

2 The way the holy prophets went—
The road that leads from banishment—
The King's highway of holiness
I'll go; for all his paths are peace.

3 This is the way I long have sought,
And mourned because I found it not;
My grief and burden long have been
Because I could not cease from sin.

4 The more I strove against its power,
I sinned and stumbled but the more,
Till late I heard my Saviour say,
" Come hither, soul, I am the Way."

5 Lo! glad I come, and Thou, bless'd Lamb,
Shalt take me to Thee as I am ;
My sinful self to Thee I give ;
Nothing but love shall I receive.

6 Then will I tell to sinners round
What a dear Saviour I have found ;
I'll point to thy redeeming blood,
And say, " Behold the way to God."

CLXXXIII.

"He that hath seen me hath seen the Father."—
John xiv. 9.

1 Our God proclaims his glorious name
Upon Mount Calvary.

Jehovah's secret name of LOVE,
'Tis there alone we see.

2 The Father's bosom who can shew,
Save his beloved Son?
Unlock the mystery of God,
And make his mercy known?

3 God is well pleased in Jesus' cross—
The cross be our delight;
The saints of God by blood redeem'd,
Are blameless in his sight.

4 At Jesus' cross we learn the song
Jehovah can approve,
We cast our crowns before his throne,
And sing " Our God is love."

CLXXXIV.

" I will love him, and will manifest myself to him."—John xiv. 21.

1 JESUS, lover of my soul,
Let me to thy bosom fly,
While the billows near me roll,
While the tempest still is high;

Hide me, O my Saviour, hide,
　Till the storm of life is past;
Safe into the haven guide,
　O receive my soul at last.

2 Other refuge have I none,
　　Hangs my helpless soul on Thee;
Leave, O leave me not alone,
　　Still support and comfort me;
All my trust on Thee is stay'd,
　　All my help from Thee I bring,
Cover my defenceless head
　　With the shadow of thy wing.

3 Thou, O Christ, art all I want,
　　Boundless love in Thee I find:
Raise the fallen, cheer the faint,
　　Heal the sick and lead the blind.
Just and holy is Thy name,
　　I am all unrighteousness;
Vile and full of sin I am,
　　Thou art full of truth and grace.

4 Plenteous grace with Thee is found,
　　Grace to pardon all my sin;

Let the healing streams abound,
  Make and keep me pure within.
Thou of life the fountain art,
  Freely let me take of Thee;
Spring thou up within my heart,
  Rise to all eternity.

CLXXXV.
"Peace I leave with you, my peace I give unto you."—John xiv. 27.

1 While to Bethlehem we are going,
    Tell me now to cheer the road;
  Tell me why this lovely Infant
    Quitted his divine abode?
      " From that world to bring to this
      Peace; which of all earthly blisses,
      Is the brightest, purest bliss."

2 Wherefore from his throne exalted,
    Came he on this earth to dwell—
  All his pomp a humble manger—
    All his court a narrow cell?
      " From that world to bring to this
      Peace; which of all earthly blisses,
      Is the brightest, purest bliss."

3 Why did he, the Lord eternal,
   Mortal pilgrim deign to be,
He who fashioned for his glory
   Boundless immortality?
    "From that world to bring to this
    Peace; which of all earthly blisses,
    Is the brightest, purest bliss."

CLXXXVI.

"Abide in me and I in you."—John xv. 4.

1 BROTHER—would'st thou Jesus see,
   And be blest by him in time?
Blest, too, in eternity?
   Brother, then abide in him.

2 Would'st thou wise and holy be,
   Be what others only seem?
Kept in sweet security?
   Brother, then abide in Him.

3 Brother, would'st thou Jesus see
   In thine heart eternally?
Then abide in Him, and He,
   Brother, will abide in thee!

4 Would'st thou all the sunshine know
   That upon a soul can beam?
   Thou hast but one thing to do,
   Brother, to abide in Him.

5 O, abide in Him, my brother,
   Give thy heart up to Him whole—
   This one thing without another
   Is sufficient for thy soul.

6 O, my brother, time is stealing,
   Swiftly, silently along;
   Soon our Lord, His love revealing,
   Shall awake our heavenly song.

7 Hallelujah, holy brother!
   Hallelujah we shall sing,
   Hallelujah, and no other,—
   Hallelujah to our King.

CLXXXVII.

"I am not alone, because the Father is with me."
—Jo. xvi. 32.

1 Quite alone, and yet not lonely,
   I'll converse with God my friend;

Now from worldly care receding,
I my time in pray'r will spend.

2 O how blessed are the moments,
When the Lord Himself draws near;
When I feel His gracious presence,
And He listens to my pray'r.

CLXXXVIII.

"Be of good cheer, I have overcome the world."
—Jo. xvi. 33.

1 Arise, ye saints, arise,
The Lord your leader is;
The foe before his banner flies,
For victory is His.

2 Lead on, Almighty Lord!
Lead on to victory,
Encouraged by the bright reward,
With joy we'll follow Thee.

3 We wait to see the day,
When toil and strife shall cease,
When we shall cast our arms away,
And dwell in endless peace.

4 This hope supports us here,
  It makes our burdens light,
  It serves our fainting hearts to cheer,
  Till faith shall end in sight.

5 Till of the prize possest,
  We hear of war no more,
  And O sweet thought! for ever rest
  On yonder peaceful shore.

CLXXXIX.

"I have declared unto them Thy name and will declare it, that the love wherewith thou hast loved me may be in them."—Jo. xvii. 26.

1 Mercy, and grace, and peace,
  Descend thro' Thee alone—
  And Thou dost all our services
  Present before the throne.

2 On us the Father's love,
  Is for thy sake bestowed;
  Thou art our Advocate above—
  Thou art our way to God.

3 Our way to God we trace,
  And thro' thy name forgiven;

From step to step, from grace to grace,
On Thee we climb to heaven.

CXC.

" Then came Jesus forth, wearing the crown of thorns, and the purple robe."—Jo. xix. 5.

1 Is that, is that thy crowning,
    The fathers' hope of old?
Is that their children's owning?
    See, see the man, behold!

2 That robe put on by scoffers—
    That reed, that thorny crown,
And He, my God! who suffers,
    Thy well-beloved Son.

3 My King! do I behold Him,
    By men derided so;
The scoffer's robe infold Him,
    And thorns his crown of woe!

4 Yet ah! 'twas I that made Him
    Thus abject and forlorn;
My sins they thus array'd Him,
    And gave Him thus to scorn.

5 Thou man of sorrows, Jesus!
　　Thy woes can we forget?
　Justice was armed to seize us,
　　But these—they paid our debt.

CXCI.

"Behold the Man."—Jo. xix. 5.

1 BEHOLD the man! how glorious He!
　　Before His foes He stands unawed,
　And without wrong or blasphemy,
　　He claims equality with God.

2 Behold the man! by all condemn'd,
　　Assaulted by a host of foes;
　His person and His claims contemn'd,
　　A man of sufferings and of woes.

3 Behold the man! He stands alone,
　　His foes are ready to devour;
　Not one of all His friends will own
　　Their Master in this trying hour.

4 Behold the man! so weak He seems,
　　His awful word inspires no fear;

But soon must He, who now blasphemes,
  Before his judgment-seat appear.

5 Behold the man ! though scorn'd below,
  He bears the greatest name above ;
The angels at His footstool bow,
  And all His royal claims approve.

CXCII.

"There stood by the cross of Jesus, His mother, and His mother's sister, Mary, the wife of Cleophas, and Mary Magdalene."—Jo. xix. 25.

1 Dear Lord, amid the throng that press'd
    Around Thee on the cursed tree,
  Some loyal, loving hearts were there,
    Some pitying eyes that wept for Thee.

2 Like them may we rejoice to own
    Our dying Lord, though crown'd with thorn ;
  Like Thee, Thy blessed self, endure
    The cross with all its joy or scorn.

3 Thy cross, Thy lonely path below,
    Show what Thy brethren all should be ;
  Pilgrims on earth, disown'd by those
    Who see no beauty, Lord, in Thee.

CXCIII.

"It is finished."—Jo. xix. 30.

1 " 'Tis finished," the Redeemer said,
And meekly bowed His dying head,
  For guilty rebels slain.
With joy we dwell upon the word,
And view thy love, victorious Lord,
  Thy wondrous love supreme.

2 Finished our righteousness and peace—
Finished our pardon and release;
  The mighty debt is paid.
By virtue of redeeming blood,
Our sins against a holy God
  Are in oblivion laid.

3 While Jesus' dying words we hear,
Blind unbelief and doubting fear,
  Have nothing to reply.
Where'er their accusations fall,
" 'Tis finished" still may answer all,
  And silence every cry.

CXCIV.

"Lovest thou me?"—Jo. xxi. 16.

1 Hark, my soul! it is the Lord,
 " 'Tis thy Saviour, hear His word;
 Jesus speaks, and speaks to thee!
 " Say, poor sinner, lov'st thou me?"

2 I deliver'd thee when bound,
 And, when bleeding, heal'd thy wound;
 Sought thee wand'ring, set thee right,
 Turn'd thy darkness into light.

3 Can a woman's tender care
 Cease toward the child she bare?
 Yes, she may forgetful be,
 Yet will I remember thee.

4 Mine is an unchanging love,
 Higher than the heights above;
 Deeper than the depths beneath,
 Free and faithful, strong as death.

5 Thou shalt see my glory soon,
 When the work of grace is done;
 Partner of my throne shalt be,
 Say, poor sinner, lov'st thou me?

6 Lord, it is my chief complaint,
That my love is weak and faint,
Yet I love Thee and adore;
O for grace to love Thee ore!

CXCV.

"Lord, thou knowest all things; Thou knowest that I love Thee."—Jo. xxi. 17.

1 I LOVE the Lord, who died for me,
I love His grace divine and free;
I love the Scriptures, there I read
Christ loved me and for me bled.

2 I love His tears and suff'rings great,
I love His precious bloody sweat,
I love His blood—were that not spilt
I could not have been freed from guilt.

3 I love to hear that He was slain,
I love his every grief and pain;
I love to meditate by faith
Upon His meritorious death.

4 I love Mount Calv'ry, where His love,
Stronger than death itself did prove;

I love to walk His mournful way,
I love the grave where Jesus lay.

5 I love His people and their ways,
I love with them to pray and praise;
I love the Father and the Son,
I love the Spirit He sent down.

6 I love to think the time will come,
When I shall be with Him at home,
And praise him in eternity,
Then shall my love completed be.

CXCVI.

"They did eat their meat with gladness, and singleness of heart."—Acts ii. 46.

1 O God, Thy bounteous hand hath spread,
  With earthly food our humble board;
And feeds our souls with sweeter bread,
  The bread of life—our dying Lord.

2 Thy grace in all things soars above
  The sweetest song Thy saints can raise;
Yet Lord, for this, and all Thy love,
  Accept our weak unworthy praise.

CXCVII.

ANOTHER OF THE SAME.

1 O Gracious Lord, be with us now,
 Supply thy children's need ;
 On Christ, the bread of life, may we
 In sweet communion feed.

2 With water from the smitten rock,
 Our thirsty spirits cheer,
 And make us all rejoice to feel
 Thy blessed presence here.

CXCVIII.

"This is the stone which was set at nought of you builders."—Acts iv. 11.

1 Hail, thou once despised Jesus !
 Hail, thou Galilean King !
 Thou didst suffer to release us ;
 Thou didst free salvation bring!
 Hail, thou agonising Saviour,
 Bearer of our sin and shame !
 By thy merits we find favour,
 Life is giv'n us through thy name.

2 Paschal Lamb, by God appointed,
    All our sins on Thee were laid!
By Almighty love anointed,
    Thou hast full atonement made,
All thy people are forgiven,
    Through the virtue of Thy blood;
Opened is the gate of Heaven;
    Peace is made 'twixt man and God.

3 Jesus, hail, enthroned in glory,
    There for ever to abide!
All the Heavenly hosts adore Thee,
    Seated at thy Father's side:
There for sinners Thou art pleading,
    There Thou dost our place prepare;
Ever for us interceding,
    'Till in glory we appear.

4 Worship, honour, power, and blessing,
    Thou art worthy to receive;
Loudest praises without ceasing
    Meet it is for us to give;
Help, ye bright angelic spirits!
    Bring your sweetest, noblest lays!
Help to sing a Saviour's merits;
    Help to chaunt Immanuel's praise.

CXCIX.

"We must, through much tribulation, enter into the kingdom of God."—Acts xiv. 22.

1 DEAR Lord! though bitter is the cup
   Thy gracious hand deals out to me,
 I cheerfully would drink it up;
   That cannot hurt which comes from Thee.

2 Mix it with Thy unchanging love;
   Let not a drop of wrath be there!
 The saints, for ever blest above,
   Were often most afflicted here.

3 From Jesus, thy incarnate Son,
   I'll learn obedience to thy will;
 And humbly kiss the chastening rod,
   When its severest strokes I feel.

CC.

ANOTHER OF THE SAME.

1 'TIS my happiness below
   Not to live without the cross,
 But the Saviour's power to know,
   Sanctifying ev'ry loss;

Trials must and will befall;
  But with humble faith to see
Love inscrib'd upon them all,
  This is happiness to me.

2 God, in Israel, sows the seeds
  Of affliction, pain, and toil;
These spring up, and choke the weeds
  Which would else o'erspread the soil:
Trials make the promise sweet,
  Trials give new life to pray'r:
Trials bring me to his feet,
  Lay me low, and keep me there.

CCI.
"I am debtor."—Rom. i. 14.

1 When this passing world is done,
When has sunk yon glaring sun,
When we stand with Christ in glory,
Looking o'er life's finished story,
Then, Lord, shall I fully know—
Not till then—how much I owe.

2 When I hear the wicked call
On the rocks and hills to fall,

When I see them start and shrink
On the fiery deluge-brink,
Then, Lord, shall I fully know—
Not till then—how much I owe.

3 When I stand before the throne,
Dressed in beauty not my own,
When I see thee as Thou art,
Love Thee with unsinning heart,
Then, Lord, shall I fully know—
Not till then—how much I owe.

4 When the praise of Heaven I hear,
Loud as thunders to the ear,
Loud as many waters' noise,
Sweet as harp's melodious voice,
Then, Lord, shall I fully know—
Not till then—how much I owe.

5 Even on earth, as through a glass
Darkly, let Thy glory pass.
Make forgiveness feel so sweet,
Make thy Spirit's help so meet,
Even on earth, Lord, make me know
Something of how much I owe.

6 Chosen not for good in me,
   Wakened up from wrath to flee,
   Hidden in the Saviour's side,
   By the Spirit sanctified :
   Teach me, Lord, on earth to show,
   By my love, how much I owe.

7 Oft I walk beneath the cloud,
   Dark as midnight's gloomy shroud;
   But, when fear is at the height,
   Jesus comes, and all is light;
   Blessed Jesus ! bid me show
   Doubting saints how much I owe.

8 When in flowery paths I tread,
   Oft by sin I'm captive led ;
   Oft I fall—but still arise—
   The Spirit comes—the tempter flies;
   Blessed Spirit ! bid me show
   Weary sinners all I owe.

9 Oft the nights of sorrow reign—
   Weeping, sickness, sighing, pain ;
   But a night Thine anger burns—
   Morning comes and joy returns ;
   God of comforts ! bid me show
   To thy poor, how much I owe.

CCII.

"Justified by faith, we have peace with God."— Rom. v. 1.

1 Lord Jesus, we believing
　In Thee have peace with God;
　Eternal life receiving,
　The purchase of Thy blood.

2 Our curse and condemnation,
　Thou barest in our stead;
　Secure is our salvation,
　In Thee our risen Head.

3 The Holy Ghost, revealing
　Thy love, hath made us blest;
　Thy stripes have given us healing;
　Upon thy love we rest.

4 In thee the Father sees us
　Accepted and complete;
　The blood from sin which frees us
　For glory makes us meet.

CCIII.

"There is now no condemnation to them which are in Christ Jesus."—Rom. viii. 1.

1 No condemnation! O my soul,
   'Tis God that speaks the word;
 Perfect in comeliness art thou,
   In Christ thy glorious Lord.

2 In heaven His blood for ever speaks
   In God the Father's ear;
 His church, the jewels, on His heart
   Jesus will ever bear.

3 No condemnation! precious word!
   Consider it, my soul,
 Thy sins were all on Jesus laid;
   His stripes have made me whole.

4 Teach us, O God, to fix our eyes
   On Christ the spotless Lamb,
 So shall we love Thy gracious will,
   And glorify thy name.

CCIV.

"The whole creation groaneth and travaileth in pain together until now."—Rom. viii. 22.

1 O WHAT a bright and blessed world
　This groaning earth of ours will be,
When from its throne the tempter hurl'd,
　Shall leave it all, O Lord, to Thee!

2 O blessed Lord! with weeping eyes,
　That blissful hour we wait to see;
While every worm or leaf that dies
　Tells of the curse and calls for Thee.

3 Come, Saviour, then, o'er all below
　Shine brightly from Thy throne above;
Bid heaven and earth Thy glory know,
　And all creation feel Thy love.

CCV.

"We know that all things work together for good to them that love God."—Rom. viii. 28.

1 WHEN heaves with sighs my anxious breast,
　In doubt if grace have made me free,
A still small voice yet whispers rest—
　And this is happiness for me!

2 When earth and hell, and this vile heart,
  To wound, destroy my soul agree,
  Through grace I act the conqueror's part—
  And this is happiness for me!

3 Wounded, perplex'd, hardly bestead,
  While from temptation's force I flee,
  God in the battle shields my head,—
  And this is happiness for me!

4 When the cold damps of death bedew
  This body wrung with agony,
  Christ shall my fainting soul renew,—
  This will be happiness for me.

CCVI.

"If God be for us, who can be against us?"—
Rom. viii. 31.

1 Is God for me, what is it
    That man can do to me?
  Oft as my God I visit,
    All woes give way and flee.

2 If God be my salvation,
    My refuge in distress,

What earthly tribulation
Can shake my stedfast peace?

3 The ground of my profession
Is Jesus and His blood,
Which gives me the possession
Of everlasting good.

4 In me and in my doing
Is nothing on this earth,
What Jesus is bestowing
Alone is truly worth.

5 My Jesus and His merit
Is all for which I care;
Were He not with my spirit,
Ah, I should soon despair.

6 I know no condemnation,
No law that speaks despair,
And Satan's accusation
I cast into the air.

7 For me there is provided
A city fair and new,
To it I shall be guided,—
Jerusalem the true!

8 My portion there is lying,
   A destined Canaan-lot;
Tho' I am daily dying,
   My Canaan withers not.

9 My heart within me leapeth,
   And cannot down be cast,
In sunshine bright it keepeth
   A never-ending feast.

10 The sun that smiling lights me,
   Is Jesus Christ alone;
And what to sing invites me,
   Is heaven on earth begun.

CCVII.

"Who is he that condemneth?"—Rom. viii. 34.

1 I REST in Christ the Son of God,
   Who took the servant's form;
By faith I flee to Jesus' cross,
   My covert from the storm.

2 At peace with God, no ills I dread,
   The cup of blessing mine;
The Lord is risen! his precious blood
   Is new and living wine.

3 Jesus put all my sins away,
  When bruis'd to make me whole;
Who shall accuse, or who condemn,
  My blameless ransom'd soul.

4 O thou destroyer, see the blood
  That makes the guilty clean;
No prey of thine, the soul on which
  This token once is seen.

CCVIII.

"Who shall separate us from the love of Christ?"
—Rom. viii. 35.

1 LORD of our hearts, beloved of Thee,
  Weary of earth, we sigh to rest,
Supremely happy, safe and free,
  For ever on Thy tender breast;
To see Thee, love Thee, feel Thee near,
  Nor dread, as now, Thy transient stay,
To dwell beyond the reach of fear,
  Lest joy should wane, or pass away.

2 Children of hope, beloved Lord!
  In Thee we live, we glory now,

Our joy, our rest, our great reward,
  Our diadem of beauty Thou!
And when exalted, Lord, with Thee,
  Thy royal throne at last we share,
To everlasting, Thou shalt be
  Our diadem, our glory, there.

CCIX.

"Now it is high time to awake out of sleep."—
    Rom. xiii. 11.

1 Bride of the Lamb! awake, awake!
    Why sleep for sorrow now?
  The hope of glory. Christ is thine,
    A child of glory, thou.

2 Thy spirit through the lonely night,
    From earthly joy apart,
  Hath sigh'd for one that's far away,
    The Bridegroom of thy heart.

3 But see, the night is waning fast,
    The breaking morn is near;
  And Jesus comes with voice of love,
    Thy drooping heart to cheer.

4 He comes, for O His yearning heart
  No more can bear delay;
  To scenes of full unmingled joy
  To call his Bride away.

5 This earth, the scene of all his woe,
  A homeless wild to thee,
  Full soon upon His heav'nly throne,
  Its rightful King shall see.

6 Thou too shalt reign—He will not wear
  His crown of joy alone;
  And earth, His royal Bride shall see
  Beside Him on the throne.

7 Then weep no more, 'tis all thine own,
  His crown, His joy divine,
  And sweeter far than all beside,
  He, He Himself is thine.

CCX.

ANOTHER OF THE SAME.

1 Gloomy and dark the night has been,
  And long the way and dreary,
  And sad each faithful saint is seen,
  And faint, and worn, and weary.

2 Ye mourning pilgrims! dry your tears,
　　And hush each sign of sorrow;
　The light of that bright morn appears,
　　The long Sabbatic morrow.

3 Lift up your heads, behold from far
　　A flood of splendour streaming;
　It is the bright and morning star,
　　In living lustre beaming.

4 And see that star-like host around,
　　Of angel-bands attending:
　Hark, hark, the trumpet's gladdening sound,
　　With shouts triumphant blending.

5 O weeping Spouse, arise, rejoice,
　　Put off thy weeds of mourning,
　And hail the Bridegroom's welcome voice
　　In triumph now returning.

CCXI.

"None of us liveth to himself, and no man dieth to himself."—Rom. xiv. 7.

1 I WILL a little pilgrim be,
　　Resolv'd alone to follow Thee,

Thou Lamb of God, who now art gone
Up to the everlasting throne.

2 I will my heart to Thee resign,
Thine only be, O be Thou mine!
The world I leave and foolish play,
To happiness to find the way.

3 My lips shall be employ'd to bless
The Lord, who is my righteousness;
My joy to serve, and praise, and love,
And then to reign with Him above.

CCXII.

"Christ our passover is sacrificed for us."—1 Cor.
v. 7.

1 Why did the paschal beast
   Of old for Israel bleed?
To be their safeguard and their feast,
   To sprinkle and to feed.

2 Dwell not my searching soul,
   On ritual shadows now;
Christ is the Lamb all pure and whole,
   The ransom'd first-born Thou.

3 Now get thy house within,
    Slay, eat, anoint thy door,
  The dread avenger comes not in
    To smite, but passeth o'er.

4 He looks and calls from high,
    Art thou to die or live?
  He hears the posts and lintels cry
    Forgive, forgive, forgive.

5 I hear the accuser roar
    Of ills that I have done;
  I know them well, and thousands more,
    Jehovah findeth none.

6 Sin, Satan, death, press near,
    To harass and appal;
  Let but my Advocate appear,
    Backward they go, and fall.

7 Before, behind, around,
    They set their fierce array,
  To fight and force me from my ground,
    Along Emmanuel's way.

8 I meet them face to face,
    Through Jesus' conquest blest;

March in the triumph of His grace,
Right onward to my rest.

9 There in His book I bear,
A more than conqueror's name—
A soldier, son, and fellow heir,
Who fought and overcame.

10 His be the victor's name,
Who fought our fight alone;
Triumphant saints no honour claim,
Their conquest was His own.

11 By weakness and defeat,
He won the meed and crown;
Trode all our foes beneath His feet,
By being trodden down.

12 He, hell, in hell laid low,
Made sin, He sin o'erthrew;
Bowed to the grave, destroyed it so,
And death, by dying, slew.

13 Bless, bless the conqueror slain,
Slain in His victory;
Who lived, who died, who lives again
For thee, His Church, for thee!

CCXIII.

"Let us keep the feast."—1 Cor. v. 8.

1 Sweet feast of love divine!
  'Tis grace that makes us free,
 To feed upon this bread and wine,
  In memory, Lord, of Thee.

2 Here every welcome guest
  Waits, Lord, from Thee to learn
 The secrets of Thy Father's breast!
  And all Thy grace discern.

3 Here conscience ends its strife,
  And faith delights to prove
 The sweetness of the bread of life,
  The fulness of Thy love.

4 That blood that flow'd for sin,
  In symbol here we see;
 And feel the blessed pledge within,
  That we are loved of Thee.

5 O, if this glimpse of love
  Is so divinely sweet,
 What will it be, O Lord above
  Thy gladd'ning smile to meet!

6 To see Thee face to face
   Thy perfect likeness wear,
  And all Thy ways of wondrous grace,
   Through endless years declare.

CCXIV.

ANOTHER OF THE SAME.

1 Jesus invites His saints
   To meet around His board;
  Here pardon'd sinners sit, and hold
   Communion with their Lord.

2 Our heavenly Father calls
   Christ and His members one;
  We are the children of His love,
   And He the first-born Son.

3 We are but several parts
   Of the same broken bread;
  The body hath its many limbs,
   But Jesus is the Head.

CCXV.

"Ye are not your own."—1 Cor. vi. 19.

1 ALL that we are, and all we have
 Shall be for ever Thine,
All that a loving heart can give
 Our cheerful hands resign.

2 For if we might make some reserve,
 If duty did not call—
Thou lovest, Lord, with such a love,
 That we would give Thee all.

CCXVI.

"This do in remembrance of me."—1 Cor. xi. 24.

1 HERE in the broken bread and wine,
 We hear him say " remember me,"
I gave my life to ransom thine,
 I bore thy curse upon the tree.

2 Lord we are Thine, we praise Thy love ;
 One with Thy saints, all one with Thee,
We would, until we meet above,
 In all our ways remember Thee.

CCXVII.

ANOTHER OF THE SAME.

1 WHILE we remember Thee,
    Lord in our midst appear,
  Let each by faith Thy body see,
    While we assemble here.

2 We never would forget
    Thy rich, Thy precious love,
  Our theme of joy and wonder here,
    Our endless song above.

3 O let Thy love constrain
    Our souls to cleave to Thee;
  And ever in our hearts remain
    That word, "remember me."

CCXVIII.

"For as often as ye eat this bread, and drink this cup, ye do shew the Lord's death till He come." —1 Cor. xi. 26.

1 MEETING in the Saviour's name,
  "Breaking bread," by His command,

To the world we thus proclaim,
　　On what ground we hope to stand,
When the Lord shall come with clouds,
Join'd by heav'n's exulting crowds.

2 From the cross our hope we draw,
　　'Tis the sinner's blest resource,
Jesus magnified the law,
　　Jesus bore its awful curse;
This the joyful truth we own,
This our ground of hope alone.

3 Jesus died and then arose,
　　Yes, He rose, He lives, He reigns,
Jesus vanquished all His foes,
　　Jesus led them all in chains;
His the triumph and the crown,
His the glory and renown.

4 Sing we then of Him who died,
　　Sing of Him who rose again,
By His blood we're justified,
　　And with Him we hope to reign,
Yes, we hope to see our Lord,
And to share His bright reward.

CCXIX.

"Some are fallen asleep."—1 Cor. xv. 6.

1 Asleep in Jesus! Blessed sleep!
From which none ever wake to weep;
A calm and undisturbed repose,
Unbroken by the last of foes!

2 Asleep in Jesus! Oh! how sweet
To be for such a slumber meet;
With holy confidence to sing,
That death has lost his venomed sting!

3 Asleep in Jesus! Peaceful rest!
Whose waking is supremely blest:
No fear, no woe, shall dim that hour
That manifests the Saviour's power.

4 Asleep in Jesus! Oh! for me
May such a blissful refuge be:
Securely shall my ashes lie,
Waiting the summons from on high.

5 Asleep in Jesus! Time nor space
Debars this precious " hiding place;"

On Indian plains or Lapland snows
Believers find the same repose.

6 Asleep in Jesus! Far from thee
Thy kindred and their graves may be;
But thine is still a blessed sleep,
From which none ever wakes to weep!

CXX.

"By the grace of God I am what I am."—1 Cor. xv. 10.

1 ALL that I *was*—my sin, my guilt,
My death was all my own;
All that I *am*, I owe to Thee,
My gracious God alone.

2 The evil of my former state,
Was mine and only mine;
The good in which I now rejoice
Is thine, and only Thine.

3 The darkness of my former state,
The bondage all was mine;
The light of life in which I walk,
The liberty is Thine.

4 Thy grace first made me feel my sin,
   It taught me to believe,
   Then, in believing, peace I found,
   And now I live, I live.

5 All that I am, even here on earth,
   All that I hope to be,
   When Jesus comes and glory dawns,
   I owe it, Lord, to Thee.

CCXXI.

"The love of Christ constraineth us."—2 Cor. v. 14.

1 My blessed Saviour, is Thy love
   So great, so full, so free?
   Behold! I give my love, my heart,
   My life, my all to Thee.

2 I love Thee for the glorious worth
   In Thy great self I see:
   I love Thee for that shameful cross
   Thou hast endured for me.

3 No man of greater love can boast,
   Than for his friend to die;

But for Thy enemies Thou wast slain;
  What love with Thine can vie?

4 Though in the very form of God,
    With heavenly glory crown'd,
  Thou wouldst partake of human flesh,
    Beset with troubles round.

5 Thou would'st like wretched man be made
    In every thing but sin;
  That we as like Thee might become,
    As we unlike have been.

6 O Lord, I'll treasure in my soul
    The memory of Thy love;
  And Thy dear name shall still to me
    A grateful odour prove.

7 Where Thou dost pitch Thy tent, and where
    Thy honour deigns to dwell,
  There I'll fix mine, and there reside,
    There Thy love's wonders tell.

CCXXII.

"Ye know the grace of our Lord Jesus Christ; that, though He was rich, yet for our sakes He became poor."—2 Cor. viii. 9.

1 THE Son of God, who fram'd the skies,
Now humbly in a manger lies;
He, who the earth's foundations laid,
A helpless infant now is made.

2 Th' eternal and Almighty God,
Assumes our feeble flesh and blood;
He deigns with sinful men to dwell,
Is God with us, Immanuel.

3 Though rich, He poor on earth became,
That we might all His riches claim,
And open'd thro' Himself, the way
To life and everlasting day.

4 For us these wonders hath He wrought,
To show His love, surpassing thought:
Then let us all unite to sing
Praise to our Saviour, God, and King.

CCXXIII.

"I am crucified with Christ."—Gal. ii. 20.

1 That "I am Thine, my Lord and God!
   Sprinkled and ransomed by Thy blood,"—
      Repeat that word once more,
   With such an energy and light,
   That this world's flattery and spite,
      To shake me never may have power.

2 From various cares my heart retires;
   Though deep and boundless its desires,
      I'm now to please but One:
   Him, before whom the elders bow,
   With Him is all my business now,
      And with the souls that are His own.

3 See! the dear flock by Jesus drawn,
   In bless'd simplicity move on;
      They trust His shepherd's crook;
   Beholders many faults will find,
   But they can tell their Saviour's mind,
      Content, if written in His book.

4 O all ye just, ye rich, ye wise,
   Who deem the atoning sacrifice,

A doctrine vain and slight;
Grant but I may (the rest's your own)
In shame and poverty sit down
At this one well-spring of delight.

5 Indeed, if Jesus was not slain,
Or ought can make His ransom vain,
That now it heals no more;
If His heart's tenderness is fled;
Were He no more the Church's head,
Nor Lord of all, as heretofore;

6 Then, (so refers my state to Him)
Unwarranted I must esteem,
And wretched all I do,
Ah, my heart throbs! and seizes fast
That covenant which will ever last;
It knows, it knows, these things are true.

7 No, my dear Lord, in following Thee,
Not in the dark, uncertainly,
This foot, obedient moves;
'Tis with a Brother and a King,
Who many to His yoke will bring,
Who ever lives and ever loves.

8 Now then my way, my truth, my life!
Henceforth let sorrow, doubt, and strife,
   Drop off like autumn leaves ;
Henceforth, as privileged by Thee,
Simple and undistracted be
   My soul which to Thy sceptre cleaves.

9 Let me my weary head recline
On that eternal love of Thine,
   And human thoughts forget ;
Child-like attend what Thou wilt say ;
Go forth and do it while 'tis day,
   Yet never leave my sweet retreat.

CCXXIV.

"Made a curse for us."—Gal. iii. 13.

1 Blessed be God, for ever blest!
   And glorious be His name!
His Son He gave, our souls to save
   From everlasting shame.

2 Nothing was precious in God's sight,
   But God's own precious blood;
Were that not shed, my guilty head
   Must bear wrath's awful load.

3 Had I worn sackcloth, and in dust
   Cast myself humbly down,
   Covered my miserable head
   With ashes for a crown.

4 These could not save me from the curse,
   Nor end the endless pain,
   Nor quench the fire, nor ease the heart,
   Nor wipe away one stain.

5 The Eternal Life His life laid down,—
   Such was the wondrous plan—
   And God, the blessed God, was made
   A curse for cursed man.

6 Our flesh He took, our sins He bore,
   Himself for us He gave.
   His cross was ours, and we with Him
   Were buried in one grave.

7 With Him we rose, with Him we live,
   With Him we sit above;
   With Him for ever we shall share
   The Father's boundless love.

8 Bless, then, Jehovah's blessed name;
   And bless our blessed King!

And songs of glad deliverance,
  For ever, ever sing!

CCXXV.

"God forbid that I should glory, save in the cross of our Lord Jesus Christ."—Gal. vi. 14.

1 When I survey the wondrous cross
   On which the Prince of Glory died,
  My richest gain I count but loss,
   And pour contempt on all my pride.

2 Forbid it, Lord, that I should boast,
   Save in the death of Christ my God:
  All the vain things that charm me most,
   I sacrifice them to His blood.

3 See from His head, His hands, His feet,
   Sorrow and love flow mingled down!
  Did e'er such love and sorrow meet,
   Or thorns compose so rich a crown?

4 His dying crimson like a robe,
   Spreads o'er His body on the tree;
  Then am I dead to all the globe,
   And all the globe is dead to me.

5 Were the whole realm of nature mine,
    That were a present far too small;
  Love so amazing, so divine,
    Demands my soul, my life, my all.

CCXXVI.

"We are members one of another."—Eph. iv. 25.

1 KINDRED in Christ, for His dear sake
    A hearty welcome here receive;
  May we together now partake
    The joys which only He can give!

2 To you and us by grace 'tis giv'n
    To know the Saviour's precious name;
  And shortly we shall meet in heav'n,
    Our hope, our way, our end the same.

3 May He, by whose kind care we meet,
    Send His good spirit from above;
  Make our communications sweet,
    And cause our hearts to burn with love!

4 Forgotten be each worldly theme,
    When Christians see each other thus:

We only wish to speak of Him
Who liv'd, and died, and reigns, for us.

5 We'll talk of all He did and said,
And suffer'd for us here below;
The path He mark'd for us to tread,
And what He's doing for us now.

6 Thus, as the moments pass away,
We'll love, and wonder, and adore,
And hasten on the glorious day,
When we shall meet to part no more.

CCXXVII.

"For we are members of His body, of His flesh, and of His bones."—Eph. v. 30.

1 Lord Jesus, are we one with Thee?
O height, O depth of love!
One with us on the cursed tree,—
We one with Thee above?

2 Such was Thy grace, that, for our sake,
Thou didst from heav'n come down!
Our mortal flesh and blood partake—
In all our misery one.

3 Our sins, our guilt, in love divine,
  Confess'd and borne by Thee;
The gall, the curse, the wrath were thine,
  To set Thy members free.

4 Ascended now, in glory bright,
  Still one with us Thou art;
Nor life, nor death, nor depth, nor height,
  Thy saints and Thee can part.

5 O teach us, Lord, to know and own
  This wondrous mystery,
That Thou with us art truly one,
  And we are one with Thee.

6 Soon, soon shall come that glorious day,
  When, seated on Thy throne,
Thou shalt to wond'ring worlds display,
  That Thou with us art one!

CCXXVIII.

"To me to live is Christ, and to die is gain."—
Phil. i. 21.

1 Lord, it belongs not to my care
  Whether I die or live;

To love and serve Thee is my share,
    And this Thy grace must give.
If life be long, I will be glad,
    That I may long obey;
If short, yet why should I be sad
    To soar to endless day?

2 Christ leads me through no darker rooms
    Than He went through before;
He that unto God's kingdom comes
    Must enter by His door.
Come, Lord, when grace has made me meet
    Thy blessed face to see;
For if thy work on earth be sweet,
    What will Thy glory be?

3 Then shall I end my sad complaints.
    And weary sinful days,
And join with the triumphant saints
    That sing Jehovah's praise.
My knowledge of that life is small,
    The eye of faith is dim;
But 'tis enough that Christ knows all,
    And I shall be with him.

CCXXIX.

*"Having a desire to depart and to be with Christ;
which is far better."*—Phil. i. 23.

1 WHAT must it be to dwell above,
   At God's right hand, where Jesus reigns,
Since the sweet earnest of His love
   O'erwhelms us on these dreary plains?
No heart can think, no tongue explain,
What bliss it is with Christ to reign!

2 When sin no more obscures the sight,
   And sorrow pains the heart no more,
How shall we view the Prince of light,
   And all His works of grace explore?
What heights, what depths of love divine
Shall there through endless ages shine!

3 This is the Heaven I long to know,
   For this I would with patience wait;
Till wean'd from earth, and all below,
   I mount to my celestial seat—
And wave my palm, and wear my crown,
And with the elders cast it down.

CCXXX.

ANOTHER OF THE SAME.

1 In yon blest plains where Jesus reigns,
   And lasting joys abound,
 I long to be, that I may see
   My Lord with glory crowned.

2 Then shall I rest upon His breast,
   And ever see His face;
 With ceaseless joy my powers employ
   In singing forth His praise.

3 O, Jesus, now one smile bestow,
   To cheer me on my way;
 In Thee I hope, hold thou me up,
   Lest I should go astray.

CCXXXI.

"He humbled Himself and became obedient unto death."—Phil. ii. 8.

1 Jesus, who lived above the sky,
  Came down to be a man and die;
  And in the Bible we may see
  How very good He used to be.

2 He went about, He was so kind,
To cure poor people who were blind,
And many who were sick and lame,
He pitied them, and did the same.

3 And, more than that, He told them too
The things that God would have them do;
And was so gentle and so mild,
He would have listened to a child.

4 But such a cruel death He died!
He was hung up and crucified!
And those kind hands that did such good,
They nailed them to a cross of wood!

5 And so He died!—and this is why
He came to be a man and die:
The Bible says He came from Heaven,
That we might have our sins forgiven.

CCXXXII.

"What things were gain to me, those I counted loss for Christ."—Phil. iii. 7.

1 Cross, reproach, and tribulation,
Ye to me are welcome guests,

When I have this consolation,
　That my soul in Jesus rests.

2 The reproach of Christ is glorious;
　Those who here his burden bear,
In the end shall prove victorious,
　And eternal glory share.

3 Christ our ever-blessed Saviour,
　　Bore for us reproach and shame;
Now as Conqueror, lives for ever,
　　And we conquer in His name.

4 Bearing the reproach of Jesus,
　　Follow Him without the gate,
Singing joyful songs and praises,
　　While ye for His glory wait.

5 Bonds, and stripes, and tribulation,
　　Are our honourable crowns;
Shame for Him is exaltation,
　　Gloomy dungeons are as thrones.

CCXXXIII.

"And be found in Him, not having mine own righteousness."—Phil. iii. 9.

1 Jesus, Thy blood and righteousness
My beauty are, my glorious dress;
'Midst flaming worlds, in these array'd,
With joy shall I lift up my head.

2 When from the dust of death I rise,
To claim my mansion in the skies,
Ev'n then shall this be all my plea,—
" Jesus hath liv'd—hath died for me."

3 Bold shall I stand in that great day;
For who ought to my charge shall lay,
If through thy blood absolv'd I am,
From sin's tremendous curse and shame?

4 This spotless robe the same appears,
When ruin'd nature sinks in years;
No age can change its glorious hue,
The robe of Christ is ever new.

CCXXXIV.

"Be careful for nothing."—Phil. iv. 6.

1 Commit thou all thy griefs
    And ways into His hands,
To His most sure and tender care
    Who earth and Heaven commands;
Who points the clouds their course,
    Whom winds and seas obey,—
He shall direct thy wand'ring feet,
    He shall prepare thy way.

2 Thou on the Lord rely,
    So safe shalt thou go on;
Fix on His word thy stedfast eye,
    So shall thy work be done;
No profit canst thou gain
    By self-consuming care;
To Him commit Thy cause; His ear
    Attends the softest prayer.

3 Thy wisdom infinite,
    Father, Thy ceaseless love
Sees all Thy children's wants, and knows
    What best for each will prove;

And whatso'er Thou will'st
  Thou dost, O King of kings;
What thine unerring wisdom chose
  Thy power to being brings.

4 Thou everywhere hast way,
  And all things serve Thy might—
Thy every act pure blessing is,
  Thy path unsullied light;
When Thou arisest, Lord,
  What shall thy word withstand?
When all Thy children want Thou giv'st;
  Who, who, shall stay Thy hand?

CCXXXV.

" Make your requests known unto God."—Phil. iv. 6.

1 GIVE to the winds thy fears,
    Hope and be undismay'd;
  God hears thy sighs, and counts thy tears,
    God shall lift up thy head.
  Through waves, and clouds, and storms,
    He gently clears the way;
  Wait thou His time, so shall this night
    Soon end in joyous day.

2 Still heavy is thy heart?
   Still sink thy spirits down?
Cast off the weight, let fear depart,
   And every care be gone;
What though thou rulest not?
   Yet Heav'n, and earth, and hell,
Proclaim God sitteth on the throne,
   And ruleth all things well.

3 Leave to His sov'reign sway
   To choose and to command,
So shalt thou, wond'ring, own His sway,—
   How wise, how strong His hand!
Far, far above thy thought
   His counsel shall appear,
When fully He the work hath wrought.
   That caus'd thy needless fear.

4 Thou seest our weakness, Lord,
   Our hearts are known to Thee;
O, lift thou up the sinking hand,
   Confirm the feeble knee:
Let us in life, in death,
   Thy stedfast truth declare,
And publish with our latest breath
   Thy love and guardian care.

CCXXXVI.

"Having made peace through the blood of His cross."—Col. i. 20.

1 THE cross, the cross, O that's my gain!
Because on that the Lamb was slain;
'Twas there my Lord was crucified,
'Twas there my Saviour for me died.

2 See what a deep-dyed red it bears,—
Look how that nail my Saviour tears!
All over stained with blood divine,
There hangs the King from David's line!

3 The stony heart dissolves in tears
When to our view the cross appears;
Christ's dying love, when truly felt,
The vilest, hardest heart doth melt.

4 Here I will stay, and gaze awhile
Upon the friend of sinners vile;
Abased, I view what I have done
To God's eternal, gracious Son.

5 Here I behold, as in a glass,
God's glory with unveiled face;

And, by beholding, I shall be
Made like to Him who loved me.

CCXXXVII.

"Ye are dead, and your life is hid with Christ in God."—Col. iii. 3.

1 With sweet contentment now we bid
 Farewell to pleasures here;
With Christ in God our life is hid,
 And all its springs are there.

2 'Tis now concealed and lodged secure
 In God's eternal Son:
From age to age it shall endure,
 Though to the world unknown.

3 Then, Lord, remove whate'er divides,
 Our lingering souls from Thee:
'Tis fit that where the Head resides
 The members too should be.

CCXXXVIII.

"Christ is all in all."—Col. iii. 11.

1 I'VE found the pearl of greatest price,
   My heart doth sing with joy;
And sing I must, a Christ I have,
   All gold without alloy.
Christ is a Prophet, Priest, and King—
   A *Prophet* full of light,
A *Priest* who stands 'twixt God and me,
   A *King* who rules with might.

2 This Christ, He is the Lord of lords,
   He is the King of kings,
He is the Sun of Righteousness
   With healing in His wings.
Christ is my meat, Christ is my drink,
   My med'cine, and my health,
My peace, my strength, my joy, my crown,
   My glory, and my wealth.

3 Christ is my Saviour, and my friend,
   My brother, yet my Lord,
My head, my hope, my counsellor,
   My advocate with God.

My Saviour is the heaven of heaven,
And what shall I Him call?
My Christ is first, my Christ is last,
My Christ is ALL in ALL.

CCXXXIX.

ANOTHER OF THE SAME.

1 Jesus is the chiefest good;
He hath sav'd us by His blood;
Let us value nought but Him,
Nothing else deserves esteem.

2 Jesus gives us life and peace,
Faith, and love, and holiness;
Ev'ry blessing, great or small,
Jesus for us purchas'd all.

3 Jesus, therefore, let us own,
Jesus we'll exalt alone;
Jesus has our sins forgiv'n;
Jesus' blood has bought us Heaven.

CCXL.

"Ye sorrow not, even as others that have no hope."—1 Thess. iv. 13.

1 MET around the sacred tomb,
   Friends of Jesus, why those tears?
'Midst this sad sepulchral gloom
   Shall your faith give way to fears?
He will soon, ev'n as He said,
Rise triumphant from the dead.

2 Hidden from all ages past,
   Was the cross's mystery,
Doubts awhile a veil had cast
   O'er that first dear family;
Till they saw Him and believ'd,
And as Lord and God receiv'd.

3 Now, with tears of love and joy,
   We remember all His pain,—
Sighs, and groans, and dying cry;
   For the Lamb for us was slain,
And, from death our souls to save,
Once for us lay in the grave.

4 Hither, sinners, all repair,
    And with Jesus Christ be dead,
All are safe from Satan's snare,
    Who to Jesus' tomb have fled;
Here the weary and opprest
Find a never-ending rest.

5 Wounded Saviour, full of grace,
    Hast thou suffered thus for me?
Ah! I hide my blushing face;
    How have I requited Thee?
Should not I with ardour burn
Some love's token to return?

6 But, alas, the spark how small!
    Scarcely seen at all to glow;
Lord, Thou know'st how short I fall,
    And my growth in grace how slow;
Yet, when to Thy cross I fly,
Soon all strange affections die.

7 In Thy death is all my trust,
    I have Thee my refuge made;
And, when once consign'd to dust,
    In the tomb my body's laid,

Then with saved souls above
I will praise Thy dying love.

8 But while here I'm left behind,
 Burden'd with infirmity,
May I help and comfort find
 Visiting Gethsemane,
Calvary, and Joseph's tomb,
Till my Sabbath's also come.

CCXLI.

"Them who sleep in Jesus will God bring with Him."—1 Thess. iv. 14.

1 THERE in peace his dust is laid,
 Jesus watches o'er his bed;
There in certain hope to lie
Till the trumpet shakes the sky.

2 One more safe;—the race is run!
Bright and brighter was the sun,
Till the shining noon-day glowed
O'er the pilgrim's heavenward road.

3 Yet a few more changing days,
Winter's cold, and sun's bright rays;

Yet a few more flowers to dress
Earth's prolific wilderness;

4 Then round the believer's tomb
Light from Heav'n shall cheer the gloom,
While the prison-house shall shake;—
First the dead in Christ shall wake.

5 Glorious hour! though sons of men
Know not how and know not when,
Lord! 'tis thine to choose the day,—
Theirs to watch, and wait, and pray.

CCXLII.

"So shall we ever be with the Lord."—1 Thess. iv. 17.

1 "For ever with the Lord;"
　　Amen, so let it be!
　Life from the dead is in that word,—
　　'Tis immortality.

2 Here, in the body pent,
　　Absent from Him I roam;
　Yet nightly pitch my moving tent
　　A day's march nearer home.

3 My Father's house on high ;
　　Home of my soul how near,—
　At times to faith's foreseeing eye
　　Thy golden gates appear!

4 Ah, then, my spirit faints
　　To reach the land I love ;
　The bright inheritance of saints,
　　Jerusalem above.

5 How shall I meet his eye?
　　Mine on the cross I cast,
　And own my life a Saviour's prize—
　　Mercy from first to last.

6 " Knowing as I am known,"—
　　How shall I love that word!
　And oft repeat before the throne,
　　" For ever with the Lord."

7 The trump of final doom
　　Shall speak the self-same word ;
　And Heav'n's voice thunder thro' the tomb,
　　" For ever with the Lord."

8 The tomb shall echo deep
　　That death-awakening sound ;

The saints shall hear it in their sleep,
And answer from the ground.

9 Then, when they upward fly,
That Resurrection-word
Shall be their shout of victory—
"For ever with the Lord."

10 That Resurrection-word,
That shout of victory,
Once more, " for ever with the Lord,"—
Amen, so let it be!

CCXLIII.

"Whether we wake or sleep, we shall live together with Him."—1 Thess. v. 10.

1 Yes, the Christian's course is run,
Ended is the glorious strife;
Fought the fight, the work is done,
Death is swallowed up of life!

2 Join we then with one accord
In the new, the joyful song;
Absent from our loving Lord
We shall not continue long.

3 We shall quit the house of clay,
   We a better lot shall share,
   We shall see the realms of day,—
   Meet our happy brother there.

4 Let the world bewail their dead,
   Fondly of their loss complain;
   Brother, friend, by Jesus freed,
   Death to thee, to us is gain!

5 Thou art enter'd into joy,
   Let the unbelievers mourn;
   We in songs our lives employ,
   Till we all to God return.

CCXLIV.

"I am now ready to be offered, and the time of my departure is at hand."—2 Tim. iv. 6.

1 I'm going to leave all my sadness,
   I'm going to change earth for Heaven;
   There, there all is peace, all is gladness,
   There pureness and glory are given,
      Come, quickly then, Jesus! Amen!

2 Friends, weep not in sorrow of spirit,
    But joy that my time here is o'er;
I go the good part to inherit,
    Where sorrow and sin are no more.
        Come quickly then, Jesus! Amen!

3 The shadows of evening are fleeing,
    Morn breaks from the city of light;
This moment day starts into being,
    Eternity bursts on my sight.
        Come quickly then, Jesus! Amen!

4 The first-born redeemed from all trouble,
    (The Lamb that was slain in the throng;)
Their ardour in praising redouble;—
    Breaks not on the ear the new song?
        Come quickly then, Jesus! Amen!

5 I'm going to tell their glad story,
    To share in their transports of praise,
I'm going in garments of glory,
    My voice to unite with their lays.
        Come quickly then, Jesus! Amen!

6 Ye fetters corrupted then leave me,
    Thou body of sin droop and die;

Pains of earth cease ye ever to grieve me,
From you 'tis for ever I fly.
Come quickly then, Jesus! Amen!

CCXLV.

"If we suffer we shall also reign with Him."—2 Tim. iv. 12.

1 JESUS, our Head, once crowned with thorns,
　Is crown'd with glory now;
　Heaven's royal diadem adorns
　The mighty victor's brow.

2 Delight of all who dwell above,
　The joy of saints below;
　To us still manifest thy love,
　That we its depths may know.

3 To us thy cross, with all its shame,
　With all its grace be given!
　Though earth disowns thy lowly name,
　All worship it in heaven.

4 Who suffer with thee, Lord, below,
　Will reign with thee above;
　Then let it be our joy to know
　This way of peace and love.

5 To us thy cross is life and health,
   Though shame and death to thee,
Our present glory, joy, and wealth,
   Our everlasting stay.

CCXLVI.

"There remaineth a rest for the people of God."
—Heb. iv. 9.

1 WE seek a rest beyond the skies,
      In everlasting day,
   Thro' floods and flames the passage lies,
      But Jesus guards the way.
   The swelling flood and raging flame,
      Hear and obey his word;
   Then let us triumph in his name,
      Our Saviour is the Lord.

CCXLVII.

"We have not an high priest which cannot be touched with the feeling of our infirmities."—Heb. iv. 15.

1 JESUS, my sorrow lies too deep
      For human ministry;

It knows not how to tell itself
   To any but to Thee.

2 Thou dost remember still, amid
   The glories of God's throne,
   The sorrows of mortality,
   For they were once thine own.

3 Yes: for, as if thou wouldst be God,
   Even in Thy misery,
   There's been no sorrow but thine own,
   Untouched by sympathy.

4 Jesus, my fainting spirit brings
   Its fearfulness to thee ;
   Thine eye, at least, can penetrate
   The clouded mystery.

5 And is it not, O Lord, enough,
   This holy sympathy ?
   There is no sorrow e'er so deep
   But I may bring to Thee.

6 It is enough, my precious Lord,
   Thy tender sympathy !
   My every sin and sorrow can
   Devolve itself on Thee.

7 As God, thou graspedst e'en the whole
    Of human misery ;—
Thine own alone lay desolate,
    That thou mightst pitied be.

8 Thy risen life but fits Thee more
    For kindly sympathy ;
Thy love unhindered rests upon
    Each bruised branch in Thee.

9 Jesus ! Thou hast availed to search
    My deepest malady;
It freely flows—more freely finds
    The gracious remedy.

CCXLVIII.

"Having obtained eternal redemption for us."—
Heb. ix. 12.

1 The atoning work is done,
    The victim's blood is shed,
And Jesus now is gone
    His people's cause to plead ;
He stands in Heaven, their great High priest,
And bears their names upon His breast.

2 He sprinkles with His blood
   The mercy-seat above;
For justice had withstood
   The purposes of love;
But justice now objects no more,
And mercy yields its boundless store.

3 No temple made with hands
   His place of service is,
In Heaven itself He stands,
   A Heavenly Priesthood his:
In Him the shadows of the law
Are all fulfill'd, and now withdraw.

4 And though awhile He be
   Hid from the eyes of men,
His people look to see
   Their great High-priest again:
In brightest glory He will come,
And take His waiting people home.

CCXLIX.

"The law having a shadow of good things to come."—Heb. x. i.

1 Israel, in ancient days,
  Not only had a view
Of Sinai in a blaze,
  But learned the gospel too:
The types and figures were a glass
In which they saw a Saviour's face.

2 The paschal sacrifice
  And blood-besprinkled door,
Seen with enlighten'd eyes,
  And once applied with pow'r,
Would teach the need of other blood
To reconcile an angry God.

3 The Lamb, the Dove, set forth
  His perfect innocence;
Whose blood of matchless worth
  Should be the soul's defence;
For He who can for sin atone
Must have no failings of His own.

4 The scape-goat on His head,
  The people's trespass bore,

And to the desert led,
  Was to be seen no more:
In Him our Surety seem'd to say,
  "Behold! I bear your sins away."

5 Dipt in his fellow's blood,
  The living bird went free;
The type well understood
  Express'd the sinner's plea,—
Describ'd a guilty soul enlarg'd,
And by a Saviour's death discharg'd.

6 Jesus, I love to trace,
  Throughout the sacred page,
The footsteps of Thy grace,
  The same in ev'ry age:
Oh, grant that I may faithful be
To clearer light vouchsaf'd to me!

CCL.

"No more conscience of sins."—Heb. x. 2.

1 Nothing but thy blood, O Jesus,
    Can relieve us from our smart;
  Nothing else from guilt release us,
    Nothing else can melt the heart.

Law and terrors do but harden,
  All the while they work alone:
But a sense of blood-bought pardon
  Soon dissolves a heart of stone.

2 Jesus, all our consolations
    Flow from Thee, the sovereign good;
  Love, and faith, and hope, and patience,
    All are purchas'd by Thy blood.
  From thy fulness we receive them,
    We have nothing of our own;
  Freely Thou delight'st to give them
    To the needy, who have none.

3 Teach us, by thy Holy Spirit,
    How to mourn, and not despair;
  Let us, leaning on thy merit,
    Wrestle hard with God in prayer.
  Whatsoe'er afflictions seize us,
    They shall profit, if not please:
  But defend, defend us, Jesus,
    From security and ease.

CCLI.

"It is not possible that the blood of bulls and of goats should take away sins."—Heb. x. 4.

1 Not all the blood of beasts,
   On Jewish altars slain,
Could give the guilty conscience peace,
   Or wash away the stain.

2 But Christ, the Heavenly Lamb,
   Takes all our guilt away;
A sacrifice of nobler name,
   And richer blood than they.

3 My faith would lay her hand
   On that dear head of Thine,
While as a penitent I stand,
   And there confess my sin.

4 My soul looks back to see
   The burdens Thou didst bear,
When hanging on the accursed tree,
   And knows her guilt was there.

5 Believing, we rejoice
   To see the curse remove;

We bless the Lamb with cheerful voice,
And sing His bleeding love.

CCLII.

"Having boldness to enter into the holiest, by the blood of Jesus, let us draw near."—Heb. x. 19-22

1 Cheer up, my soul, there is a mercy-seat
    Sprinkled with blood, where Jesus answers pray'r;
  There humbly cast thyself beneath His feet,
    For never needy sinner perish'd there.

2 Lord, I am come! Thy promise is my plea,
    Without Thy word I durst not venture nigh;
  But Thou hast called the burden'd soul to Thee,
    A weary burden'd soul, O Lord, am I!

3 Bow'd down beneath a heavy load of sin,
    By Satan's fierce temptations sorely prest,
  Beset without, and full of fears within,
    Trembling and faint, I come to Thee for rest.

4 Be Thou my refuge, Lord, my hiding-place,
    I know no force can tear me from Thy side;

Unmov'd, I then may all accusers face,
And answer ev'ry charge, with "Jesus died."

5 Yes, Thou didst weep, and bleed, and groan, and die,
Well hast Thou known what fierce temptations mean;
Such was Thy love; and now, enthron'd on high,
The same compassions in Thy bosom reign.

6 Lord, give me faith—he hears—what grace is this!
Dry up thy tears, my soul, and cease to grieve;
He shows me what He did, and who He is,
I must, I will, I can, I do believe.

CCLIII.

"Now they desire a better country, that is an Heavenly."—Heb. xi. 16.

1 WITH Heaven in view, we tread the path
The saints of former ages trod;
Like them the children once of wrath,
But now, like Christ, the sons of God.

2 No room for any boast have we;
Upon another's wealth we live;

The pardon we enjoy is free,
The praise to God alone we give.

3 We seek a city far from this,
A distant city, out of sight;
Our God himself its builder is—
The Lamb its everlasting light.

4 And sad to us the way appears,
Till we our Lord and God shall see;
Yet though while here we sow in tears,
Our harvest hence e'er long shall be.

CCLIV.

"He hath prepared for them a city."—Heb. xi. 16.

1 JERUSALEM, my happy home!
Name ever dear to me!
When shall my labors have an end,
In joy, and peace, and thee?

2 When shall these eyes thy heaven-built walls,
And pearly gates behold?
Thy bulwarks with salvation strong,
And streets of shining gold?

3 O when, thou city of my God,
   Shall I Thy courts ascend,
   Where congregations ne'er break up,
   And Sabbaths have no end?

4 There happier bowers than Eden's bloom,
   Nor sin nor sorrow know,
   Bless'd seats! thro' rude and stormy scenes
   I onward press to you.

5 Why should I shrink at pain and woe,
   Or feel at death dismay?
   I've Canaan's goodly land in view,
   And realms of endless day.

6 Apostles, Martyrs, Prophets, there
   Around my Saviour stand,
   And soon my friends in Christ below,
   Will join the glorious band.

7 Jerusalem! my happy home,
   My soul still pants for thee,
   Then shall my sorrows have an end,
   When I thy joys shall see.

CCLV.

ANOTHER OF THE SAME.

1 I'm but a stranger here—
 Heaven is my home.
Earth is a desert drear—
 Heaven is my home.
Danger and sorrow stand
Round me on every hand;
Heaven is my Fatherland—
 Heaven is my home.

2 What though the tempests rage—
 Heaven is my home;
Short is my pilgrimage—
 Heaven is my home.
And time's wild wintry blast
Soon shall be over past;
I shall reach home at last—
 Heaven is my home.

3 There, at my Saviour's side—
 Heaven is my home;
I shall be glorified—
 Heaven is my home.

There are the good and blest,
Those I loved most and best,
And there I too shall rest—
  Heaven is my home.

4 Therefore I murmur not—
  Heaven is my home.
Whate'er my earthly lot—
  Heaven is my home.
And I shall surely stand
There at my Lord's right hand;
Heaven is my Fatherland—
  Heaven is my home.

CCLVI

"God having provided some better thing for us."
—Heb. xi. 40.

1 O, WHAT a lonely path were ours,
  Could we, O Father, see
No home of rest beyond it all,
  No guide or help in Thee!

2 But Thou art near, and with us still,
  To keep us on the way

The pardon we enjoy is free,
The praise to God alone we give.

3 We seek a city far from this,
A distant city, out of sight;
Our God himself its builder is—
The Lamb its everlasting light.

4 And sad to us the way appears,
Till we our Lord and God shall see;
Yet though while here we sow in tears,
Our harvest hence e'er long shall be.

CCLIV.

"He hath prepared for them a city."—Heb. xi. 16.

1 JERUSALEM, my happy home!
Name ever dear to me!
When shall my labors have an end,
In joy, and peace, and thee?

2 When shall these eyes thy heaven-built walls,
And pearly gates behold?
Thy bulwarks with salvation strong,
And streets of shining gold?

3 O when, thou city of my God,
   Shall I Thy courts ascend,
   Where congregations ne'er break up,
   And Sabbaths have no end?

4 There happier bowers than Eden's bloom,
   Nor sin nor sorrow know,
   Bless'd seats! thro' rude and stormy scenes
   I onward press to you.

5 Why should I shrink at pain and woe,
   Or feel at death dismay?
   I've Canaan's goodly land in view,
   And realms of endless day.

6 Apostles, Martyrs, Prophets, there
   Around my Saviour stand,
   And soon my friends in Christ below,
   Will join the glorious band.

7 Jerusalem! my happy home,
   My soul still pants for thee,
   Then shall my sorrows have an end,
   When I thy joys shall see.

CCLV.

ANOTHER OF THE SAME.

1 I'm but a stranger here—
    Heaven is my home.
Earth is a desert drear—
    Heaven is my home.
Danger and sorrow stand
Round me on every hand;
Heaven is my Fatherland—
    Heaven is my home.

2 What though the tempests rage—
    Heaven is my home;
Short is my pilgrimage—
    Heaven is my home.
And time's wild wintry blast
Soon shall be over past;
I shall reach home at last—
    Heaven is my home.

3 There, at my Saviour's side—
    Heaven is my home;
I shall be glorified—
    Heaven is my home.

There are the good and blest,
Those I loved most and best,
And there I too shall rest—
　Heaven is my home.

4 Therefore I murmur not—
　Heaven is my home.
Whate'er my earthly lot—
　Heaven is my home.
And I shall surely stand
There at my Lord's right hand;
Heaven is my Fatherland—
　Heaven is my home.

CCLVI

"God having provided some better thing for us."
　—Heb. xi. 40.

1 O, WHAT a lonely path were ours,
　Could we, O Father, see
No home of rest beyond it all,
　No guide or help in Thee!

2 But Thou art near, and with us still,
　To keep us on the way

2 Forth from His Father's loving breast,
   To bear our sin and shame,
To face a cold unfeeling world
   The Heavenly stranger came.

3 This earth to Him, the Lord of all,
   No kindly welcome gave;
In Judah's land the Saviour found
   No shelter but the grave.

4 Then fare thee well, thou faithless world!
   Thine evil eye could see
No grace in Him, whose dying love
   Hath weaned our hearts from Thee.

5 The cross was His; and O, 'tis ours
   Its weight on earth to bear,
And glory in the thought that He
   Was once a sufferer there.

CCLX.

"We seek one to come."—Heb. xiii. 14

1 This is not my place of resting,
   Mine's a city yet to come;

Onwards to it I am hasting,—
On to my eternal home.

2 In it all is light and glory,
O'er it shines a nightless day ;
Every trace of sin's sad story,—
All the curse has pass'd away.

3 There the Lamb, our Shepherd, leads us
By the streams of life along ;
On the freshest pastures feeds us,
Turns our sighing into song.

4 Soon we pass this desert dreary,
Soon we bid farewell to pain ;
Never more be sad or weary,
Never, never sin again.

CCLXI.

"Let patience have her perfect work."—Jas. i. 4.

1 Tho' the heart that sorrow chideth
Sink in anguish and in care ;
Yet, if patience still abideth,
Hope shall paint her rainbow there.

2 Faith's bright lamp her light shall borrow
From religion's blessed ray,

And from every coming morrow
Charm the clouds of grief away.

3 Wherefore should we sigh and languish,
When our cares so soon shall cease,
And the heart that sows in anguish
Shall hereafter reap in peace?

4 This is not a scene of pleasure,
These are not the shores of bliss;
We shall gain a brighter treasure,
Find a dearer land than this.

CCLXII.

"What is your life? It is even a vapour."—Jas. iv. 14.

1 Like mist on the mountain, like ships on the sea,
So swiftly the years of our pilgrimage flee;
In the grave of our fathers how soon we shall lie!
Dear children, to-day to a Saviour fly.

2 How sweet are the flow'rets of April and May!
But often the frost makes them wither away;
Like flowers you may fade!—are you ready to die?
While yet there is room, to a Saviour fly.

3 When Samuel was young he first knew the Lord—
He slept in His smile and rejoiced in His word;
So most of God's children are early brought nigh;
Oh, seek Him in youth,—to a Saviour fly!

4 Do you ask me for pleasure? Then lean on His breast,
For there the sin-laden and weary find rest,
In the valley of death you will triumphing cry,
If this be called dying, 'tis pleasant to die.

CCLXIII.

"The sufferings of Christ and the glory that should follow."—1 Pet. i. 11.

1 To Calv'ry, Lord, in spirit now
   Our weary souls repair;
To dwell upon Thy dying love,
   And taste its sweetness there.

2 Sweet resting-place of every heart
   That feels the plague of sin,
Yet knows the deep mysterious joy
   Of peace with God within.

3 There, through thine hour of deepest woe,
   Thy suffering spirit pass'd;

Grace there its wondrous victory gain'd,
  And love endured its last.

4 Dear suffering Lamb! Thy bleeding wounds,
    With cords of love divine,
  Have drawn our willing hearts to Thee,
    And link'd our life with thine.

5 Thy sympathies and hopes are ours;
    Dear Lord! we wait to see
  Creation, all below, above,
    Redeem'd and blest by Thee.

6 Our longing eyes would fain behold
    That bright and blessed brow,
  Once wrung with bitterest anguish, wear
    Its crown of glory now.

7 Why linger then? Come, Saviour, come,
    Responsive to our call;
  Come, claim thine ancient power, and reign,
    The heir and Lord of all.

CCLXIV.

"Christ also suffered for us, leaving us an example that we should follow His steps."—1 Pet. ii. 21.

1 O Lord, when we the path retrace,
    Which Thou on earth hast trod;
  To man Thy wondrous love and grace,
    Thy faithfulness to God:
  Thy love, by man so sorely tried,
    Proved stronger than the grave;
  The very spear that pierc'd Thy side
    Drew forth the blood to save.

2 Faithful amidst unfaithfulness,
    'Midst darkness only light,
  Thou didst Thy Father's name confess,
    And in His will delight.
  Unmoved by Satan's subtle wiles,
    Or suffering, shame and loss:
  Thy path, uncheer'd by earthly smiles,
    Led only to the cross.

3 O Lord, with sorrow and with shame,
    Before Thee we confess
  How little we, who bear Thy name,
    Thy mind, Thy ways express.

Give us Thy meek, Thy lowly mind;
We would obedient be;
And all our rest and pleasure find,
In learning, Lord, of Thee.

CCLXV.

"Leaving us an example, that ye should follow His steps."—1 Pet. ii. 21.

1 LAMB of God, I look to Thee,
Thou shalt my example be;
When Thou wast a little child,
Thou wast gentle, meek, and mild.

2 Due obedience Thou didst show,
O, make me obedient too;
Thou wast merciful and kind,
Grant me, Lord, Thy loving mind.

3 Let me, above all, fulfil
God, my heav'nly Father's will;
Never His good Spirit grieve—
Only to His glory live.

4 Loving Jesus, holy Lamb,
In Thy hands secure I am;

Fix Thy temple in my heart,
Never from Thy child depart.

5 Teach me to show forth Thy praise,
Love and serve Thee all my days:
Oh, might all around me see
Christ, the Holy Child, in me!

CCLXVI.

"Ye were as sheep going astray; but are now returned unto the Shepherd and Bishop of your souls."—1 Pet. ii. 25.

1 I was a wand'ring sheep,
   I did not love the fold;
   I did not love my Shepherd's voice,
   I would not be controll'd.
I was a wayward child,
   I did not love my home;
   I did not love my Father's voice,
   I loved afar to roam.

2 The Shepherd sought His sheep,
   The Father sought His child;
   They followed me o'er vale and hill,
   O'er deserts waste and wild.

  They found me nigh to death,
   Famished, and faint, and lone;
  They bound me with the bands of love·
   They saved the wandering one!

3 They spoke in tender love,
  They raised my drooping head;
 They gently closed my bleeding wounds,
  My fainting soul they fed.
 They washed my filth away,
  They made me clean and fair;
 They brought me to my home in peace;
  The long-sought wanderer!

4 Jesus my Shepherd is,
  'Twas He that loved my soul,
 'Twas He that washed me in His blood,
  'Twas He that made me whole.
 'Twas He that sought the lost,
  That found the wandering sheep,
 'Twas He that brought me to the fold—
  'Tis He that still doth keep.

5 I was a wandering sheep,
  I would not be controll'd:

But now I love my Shepherd's voice,
I love, I love the fold!
I was a wayward child;
I once preferr'd to roam;
But now I love my Father's voice—
I love, I love His home!

CCLXVII.

"To Him be glory, both now and for ever."—2 Pet. iii. 18.

1 WE sing the praise of Jesus, the holy Lamb of God,
Who came from Heaven to bless us, and shed for us His blood;
Who died in awful anguish, upon the cross, that we
Might live to sing His praises throughout eternity.

2 We sing the praise of Jesus, tho' once on earth He taught,
He's now in Heaven and sees us, and knows our every thought;
He will not frown upon us, altho' to Him we raise
Our sinful hearts and voices, in one sweet song of praise.

3 We sing the praise of Jesus, who did our souls redeem,
Who welcomed little children when they were brought to Him ;
He kindly spoke, and told them that they for Him had charms,
And then He did enfold them, and bless'd them, in His arms.

CCLXVIII.

"If we walk in the light, as He is in the light, we have fellowship one with another."—1 Jo. i. 7.

1 Walk in the light ! so shalt thou know,
That fellowship of love,
His Spirit only can bestow
Who reigns in light above.
Walk in the light ! and sin abhorred
Shall ne'er defile again ;
The blood of Jesus Christ the Lord,
Shall cleanse from every stain.

2 Walk in the light! and thou shalt find
Thy heart made truly His,
Who dwells in cloudless light enshrined,
In whom no darkness is.

Walk in the light! and thou shalt own
  Thy darkness passed away,
Because that light hath on thee shone,
  In which is perfect day.

3 Walk in the light! and e'en the tomb
  No fearful shade shall wear;
Glory shall chase away its gloom,
  For Christ hath conquer'd there!
Walk in the light! and thou shalt see
  A path, tho' thorny, bright;
For God, by grace, shall dwell in thee,
  And God himself is light.

CCLXIX.

"The darkness is past, and the true light now shineth."—1 Jo. ii. 8.

1 'Tis past—the dark and dreary night,
  And, Lord, we hail Thee now,
Our Morning Star, without a cloud
  Of sadness on Thy brow.
Thy path on earth, the cross, the grave,
  Thy sorrows all are o'er;
And oh! sweet thought! thy eye shall weep,
  Thy heart shall break no more.

2 Deep were those sorrows—deeper still
    The love that brought thee low;
  That bade the streams of life from Thee,
    A willing victim, flow.
  The soldier, as he pierc'd Thee, prov'd
    Man's hatred, Lord, to Thee;
  While in the blood that stain'd the spear,
    Love, only love we see.

3 Drawn from Thy pierc'd and bleeding side,
    That pure and cleansing flood,
  Speaks peace to every heart that knows
    The virtues of Thy blood.
  Yet, 'tis not that we know the joy
    Of cancell'd sin alone,
  But, happier far, Thy saints are call'd
    To share Thy glorious throne.

4 So closely are we link'd in love,
    So wholly one with Thee,
  That all *Thy* bliss and glory then
    Our bright reward shall be.
  Yes, when the storm of life is calm'd—
    The weary desert pass'd,
  Our way-worn hearts shall find in Thee
    Their full repose at last.

CCLXX.
*"Abide in Him."—*1 Jo. ii. 28.

1 CLING to the Crucified!
His death is life to thee,—
Life for eternity,
His pains thy pardon seal;
His stripes thy bruises heal;
His cross proclaims thy peace,
Bids every sorrow cease.
His blood is all to thee,
   It purges thee from sin;
It sets thy spirit free,
   It keeps thy conscience clean,
Cling to the Crucified!

2 Cling to the Crucified!
His is a heart of love,
Full as the hearts above;
Its depths of sympathy
Are all awake for thee.
His countenance is light,
Even in the darkest night.
That love shall never change,
   That light shall ne'er grow dim;
Charge thou thy faithless heart

To find its all in Him.
Cling to the Crucified!

CCLXXI.

"We shall see him as He is."—1 Jo. iii. 2.

1 For ever to behold Him shine,
　For evermore to call Him mine,
　　And see Him still before me!
　For ever on His face to gaze,
　And meet His full assembled rays,
　While all the Father He displays
　　To all the saints in glory!

2 Not all things else are half so dear
　As His delightful presence here—
　　What must it be in Heaven!
　'Tis Heav'n on earth to hear Him say,
　As now we journey day by day,
　" Poor sinner, cast thy fears away,
　　Thy sins are all forgiven."

3 But how will His celestial voice
　Make our enraptur'd hearts rejoice
　　When we in glory hear Him!

While we no longer at the gate,
But in His blessed presence wait,
And Jesus, on His throne of state,
Invites us to come near Him.

CCLXXII.
"Herein is love."—1 Jo. iv. 10.

1 O BLESSED love! were thou but known,
   Men would enjoy a calm repose;
But, as a labour of their own,
   They toil, and none thy sweetness knows.

2 O love! would all submit to give
   To Thee the honour of the whole;
How gladly wouldst Thou all forgive,
   Be all in all to every soul.

CCLXXIII.
"As He is, so are we in this world."—1 Jo. iv. 17.

1 A PILGRIM through this lonely world
   The blessed Saviour pass'd;
A mourner all His life was He,
   A dying Lamb at last.

That tender heart that felt for all,
    For us its life-blood gave;
It found on earth no resting-place,
    Save only in the grave.

2 Such was our Lord—and shall we fear
    The cross with all its scorn?
Or love a faithless evil world
    That wreathed his brow with thorn?
No—facing all its frowns or smiles,
    Like Him obedient still,
We homeward press, thro' storm or calm,
    To Zion's blessed hill.

3 In tents we dwell, amid the waste,
    Nor turn aside to roam
In folly's paths, nor seek our rest
    Where Jesus had no home.
Dead to the world, with Him who died
    To win our hearts—our love,
We, risen with our risen Head,
    In spirit dwell above.

4 By faith, His boundless glories there
    Our wond'ring eyes behold,
Those glories which eternal years
    Shall never all unfold.

This fills our hearts with deep desire
To lose ourselves in love,
Bears all our hopes from earth away,
And fixes them above.

CCLXXIV.

"We love Him, because He first loved us."—1 Jo. iv. 19.

1 IF human kindness meets return,
And owns the grateful tie;
If tender thoughts within us burn,
To feel a friend is nigh,—

2 O! shall not warmer accents tell
The gratitude we owe
To Him who died our fears to quell,—
Our more than orphan's woe!

3 While yet His anguish'd soul survey'd
Those pangs He would not flee;
What love His latest words display'd,
" Meet and remember Me!"

4 Remember Thee, Thy death, Thy shame,
Our sinful hearts to share!

O memory, leave no other name
But his recorded there.

CCLXXV.

"Unto Him that first loved us, and washed us from our sins in His own blood, to Him be glory and dominion."—Rev. i. 5, 6.

1 Now, let us join with heart and tongues,
To imitate the angels' songs;
Yea, sinners may address their King
In songs that angels cannot sing.
They praise the Lamb that once was slain,
But *we* can add a higher strain,
Not only say, " He suffered thus,"
But, " that He suffered all for us !"

2 Jesus, who pass'd the angels by,
Assum'd our flesh to bleed and die;
And still He makes it His abode,
As man He fills the throne of God.
Our next of kin, our Brother now,
Is He to whom the angels bow;
They join with us to praise His name,
But we the nearest interest claim.

3 But, ah! how faint our praises rise!
Sure, 'tis the wonder of the skies,
That we who share His richest love,
So cold and unconcern'd should prove,
O glorious hour! it comes with speed!
When we, from sin and darkness freed,
Shall see that God who died for man,
And praise Him more than angels can!

CCLXXVI.

ANOTHER OF THE SAME.

1 On earth the song begins,
    In Heav'n more sweet and loud,
  " To Him that cleans'd our sins
    By His atoning blood;
  " To Him," they sing, in joyful strain,
  " Be honour, pow'r, and praise, Amen."

2 Believers now repeat
    What Heav'n with gladness owns;
  And, while before His feet
    The elders cast their crowns,
  Go, imitate the choirs above,
  And sing aloud the Saviour's love.

3   Alone He bore the cross,
      Alone its grief sustain'd;
    His was the shame and loss,
      And He the victory gain'd;
    The mighty work was all His own,
    And He shall ever wear the crown.

CCLXXVII.

"Behold He cometh with clouds, and every eye shall see Him."—Rev. i. 7.

1 Lo! He comes, with clouds descending,
    Once for favour'd sinners slain!
  Thousand, thousand saints attending,
    Swell the triumph of His train,
      Hallelujah!
    Jesus comes on earth to reign!

2 Every eye shall now behold Him,
    Rob'd in dreadful majesty;
  Those who set at nought and sold Him,
    Pierc'd and nail'd Him to the tree,
      Deeply wailing,
    Shall the true Messiah see.

3 When the solemn trump has sounded,
   Heaven and earth shall flee away,
   All who hate Him must, confounded,
   Hear the summons of that day;
     Come to judgment!
   Come to judgment! come away!

4 Now redemption long expected,
   See in solemn pomp appear,
   All His saints, by man rejected,
   Rise to meet Him in the air;
     Hallelujah!
   See the day of God appear!

5 Answer thine own Bride and Spirit,
   Hasten, Lord, the general doom;
   The new Heaven and earth t'inherit,
   Take thy pining exiles home;
     All creation
   Travails, groans, and bids Thee come!

6 Yea, amen! let all adore Thee,
   High on thine eternal throne!
   Saviour! take the power and glory,
   Make thy righteous sentence known;

O, come quickly,
Claim the kingdoms for Thine own!

CCLXXVIII.

"I am He that liveth, and was dead."—Rev. i. 18.

1 SWEET is the savour of His name
   Who suffer'd in His people's stead;
  His portion here, reproach and shame:
   He liveth now; He once was dead.

2 *He once was dead;* the very same
   Who sits on yonder throne above;
  Who bears in Heaven the greatest name—
   Whom angels serve, whom angels love.

3 *He once was dead;* the very same
   Who made the worlds—a work of power;
  Who now upholds the mighty frame,
   And keeps it to the final hour.

4 *He once was dead;* but now he lives,
   His glory fills all Heaven above;
  Its blessedness to Heaven He gives—
   The fountain He of joy and love.

5 His people shall his triumph share,
    With Him shall live, with Him shall reign,
  In Heaven their joy is full, for there
    They see THE LAMB for sinners slain.

CCLXXIX.

"Nevertheless, I have somewhat against thee, because thou hast left thy first love."—Rev. ii. 4.

1 O, WHERE is now that glowing love
    That mark'd our union with the Lord?
  Our hearts were fix'd on things above,
    Nor could the world a joy afford.

2 Where is the zeal that led us then
    To make our Saviour's glory known;
  That freed us from the fear of men,
    And kept our eye on Him alone?

3 Where are the happy seasons spent
    In fellowship with Him we loved?
  The sacred joy, the sweet content,
    The blessedness that then we proved?

4 Behold, again we turn to Thee,
    O cast us not away, though vile!

No peace we have, no joy we see,
O Lord, our God, but in Thy smile.

CCLXXX.

"I will give Him the morning Star."—Rev. ii. 28.

1 There is a morning Star, my soul,
There is a morning Star;
'Twill soon be near and bright, tho' now
It seems so dim and far.
And when time's stars have come and gone,
And every mist of earth has flown,
That better star shall rise
On this world's clouded skies,
To shine for ever!

2 The night is well nigh spent, my soul,
The night is well nigh spent,
And soon above our heads shall shine
A glorious firmament;
Unutterably pure and bright,
The Lamb, once slain, its perfect light,
A light unchanging and divine,
A star that shall unclouded shine,
Descending never!

CCLXXXI.

"As many as I love I rebuke and chasten."—
Rev. iii. 19.

1 OFTEN the clouds of deepest woe
    So sweet a message bear,
  Dark tho' they seem, 'twere hard to find
    A frown of anger there.

2 Kind, loving is the hand that strikes,
    However keen the smart,
  If sorrow's discipline can chase
    One evil from the heart.

3 He was a man of sorrows—He
    Who lov'd and sav'd us thus;
  And shall the world, that frown'd on Him,
    Wear only smiles for us?

4 No; we must follow in the path
    Our Lord and Saviour run;
  We must not find a resting-place,
    Where He we love had none.

CCLXXXII.

"Behold I stand at the door and knock."—Rev. iii. 20.

1 How long the time since Christ began
    To call in vain on me!
  Deaf to His warning voice, I ran
    Through paths of vanity.

2 He called me when my thoughtless prime
    Was early ripe to ill;
  I passed from folly on to crime,
    And yet He called me still.

3 He called me in the time of dread,
    When death was full in view,
  I trembled on my feverish bed,
    Yet rose to sin anew.

4 Yet, could I hear Him once again,
    As I have heard of old,
  Methinks He should not call in vain
    His wanderer to the fold!

5 O Thou that every thought dost know,
    And answerest every prayer,

Try me with sickness, want, and woe,
But snatch me from despair!

6 My struggling will by grace control,
Renew my broken vow,—
What blessed light breaks on my soul,—
My God! I hear thee now!

CCLXXXIII.

"Thou art worthy, O Lord, to receive glory, and honour, and power."—Rev. iv. 11.

1 GLORY, glory everlasting,
  Be to Him who bore the cross,
Who redeem'd our souls by tasting
  Death—the death deserved by us;
    Spread His glory,
Who redeem'd His people thus.

2 His is love—'tis love unbounded,
  Without measure, without end;
Human thought is here confounded,
  'Tis too vast to comprehend;
    Praise the Saviour!
Magnify the sinner's friend!

3 While we hear the wondrous story
    Of the Saviour's cross and shame,
  Sing we " Everlasting glory
    Be to God and to the Lamb;"
  Saints and angels
  Give ye glory to His name.

CCLXXXIV.

ANOTHER OF THE SAME.

1 Thou, great Redeemer, dying Lamb!
    We love to hear of Thee;
  No music's like Thy precious name,
    Nor half so sweet can be.

2 Our Jesus shall be still our theme,
    While in this world we stay:
  We'll sing our Jesus' blessed name,
    When all things else decay.

3 When we appear in yonder cloud,
    With all Thy favour'd throng,
  Then will we sing more sweet, more loud,
    And Christ shall be our song.

CCLXXXV.

"I beheld, and, lo! in the midst of the throne stood a Lamb as it had been slain."—Rev. v. 6.

1 BEHOLD the Lamb, with glory crown'd!
To Him all power is given:
No place too high for Him is found,
Even in the highest Heaven.

2 This song be ours, and this alone,
That celebrates the name
Of Him who sitteth on the throne,
And that exalts the Lamb.

3 To Him whom men despise and slight,
To Him be glory given:
The crown is His; and His by right
The highest place in Heaven.

CCLXXXVI.

"Blessing, and honour, and glory, be unto the Lamb for ever and ever."—Rev. v. 13.

1 AWAKE, and sing the song,
Of Moses and the Lamb,
Wake ev'ry heart, and ev'ry tongue,
To praise the Saviour's name.

2   Sing of His dying love,
    Sing of His rising pow'r,
  Sing how He intercedes above,
    For those whose sins He bore.

3   Soon shall we hear him say,
    " Ye ransom'd sinners, Come ;"
  Soon will He call us hence away,
    And take His pilgrims home.

4   There shall each raptur'd tongue
    His nobler praise proclaim ;
  And sweeter voices tune the song
    Of Moses and the Lamb.

CCLXXXVII.

"They ascended up to Heaven in a cloud."—
Rev. xi. 12.

1 Far from home, I feel a longing ;
    Earth is but a barren clod ;
  While the storms are round me thronging,
    Take, oh take me home to God.

2 Part, ye clouds of earth, asunder,
    Now I rise from this dull sod ;

Jesus, Lord, receive me yonder—
Take, oh take me home to God.

CCLXXXVIII.

" These are they that follow the Lamb whithersoever He goeth."—Rev. xiv. 4.

1 YE blest domestics of the slaughter'd Lamb;
Ye joint partakers of illustrious shame;
Ye twigs and branches of that standard wood;
Ye stout asserters that the Lamb is God!

2 Ye who by nature cursed sinners were,
But now of sons and heirs the glory share;
Ye who have found sweet rest in Jesus' smart,
More or less happy as ye know His heart!

3 Ye who would rather live, and fight awhile,
Than be dismiss'd, as yet, from glorious toil;
Who from the world's bewitching lusts are fled,
And burn to advance the glory of your Head!

4 Before the Lamb once slain, come bow the knee,
First-born of all the first-born family;
Learn from His lips your path on earth below,
And then, in this your strength, go, warriors, go!

5 At thy command we go, or here or there,—
Many commands, as many conquests are!
Speak but the word, all obstacles must flee,
Here moves a mountain, there divides a sea!

CCLXXXIX.

" They are without fault before the throne of God.'
—Rev. xiv. 5.

1 Had I a throne above the rest,
   Where angels and archangels dwell;
One sin, unslain, within my breast,
   Would make that Heaven as dark as hell.

2 The pris'ner sent to breathe fresh air,
   And bless'd with liberty again,
Would mourn were he condemn'd to wear
   One link of all his former chain.

3 But oh! no foe invades the bliss
   When glory crowns the Christian's head;
One view of Jesus as He is,
   Will strike all sin for ever dead.

CCXC.

"Blessed are the dead which die in the Lord."—
Rev. xiv. 13.

1 In vain our fancy strives to paint
The moment after death,
The glories that surround the saint,
When he resigns his breath.

2 One gentle sigh his fetters breaks;
We scarce can say, "he's gone,"
Before the willing spirit takes
Her mansion near the throne.

3 Faith strives, but all its efforts fail
To trace her heavenward flight;
No eye can pierce within the veil,
Which hides that world of light.

4 Thus much, (and this is all) we know,
They are supremely blest;
Have done with sin, and care, and woe,
And with their Saviour rest.

5 On harps of gold His name they praise,
His presence always view;

And if we *here* their footsteps trace,
There we shall praise Him too.

CCXCI.

"On his head were many crowns."—Rev. xix. 12.

1 ALL hail the power of Jesus' name!
   Let angels prostrate fall;
  Bring forth the royal diadem,
   And crown Him Lord of all.

2 Crown Him, ye martyrs of your God,
   Who from His altar call;
  Extol the stem of Jesse's rod,
   And crown Him Lord of all.

3 Ye chosen seed of Israel's race,
   A remnant weak and small,
  Hail Him who saves you by His grace,
   And crown Him Lord of all.

4 Ye Gentile sinners, ne'er forget
   The wormwood and the gall;
  Go, spread your trophies at His feet,
   And crown Him Lord of all.

5 Let every kindred, every tribe,
    On this terrestrial ball,
  To Him all majesty ascribe,
    And crown Him Lord of all.

6 O that, with yonder sacred throng,
    We at His feet may fall;
  There join the everlasting song,
    And crown Him Lord of all.

CCXCII.

"And the armies which were in Heaven followed Him."—Rev. xix. 14.

1 Lo, 'tis the Heavenly army,
    The Lord of Hosts attending,
      'Tis He—the Lamb,
      The great I AM,
    With all His saints descending.
  To you, ye kings and nations,
  Ye foes of Christ, assembling;
      The hosts of light,
      Prepared for fight,
    Come with the cup of trembling.

2 Joy to His ancient people!
  Your bonds He comes to sever,—
    And now, 'tis done!
    The Lord hath won,
  And ye are free for ever.
  Joy to the ransom'd nations!
  The foe, the rav'ning lion,
    Is bound in chains
    While Jesus reigns,
  King of the earth, in Zion.

3 Joy to the Church triumphant,
  The Saviour's throne surrounding!
    They see His face,
    Adore His grace,
  O'er all their sin abounding:
  Crown'd with the mighty victor,
  His royal glory sharing;
    Each fills a throne,
    His name alone
  To Heaven and earth declaring.

4 Praise to the Lamb for ever!
  Bruised for our sin, and gory,
    Behold His brow,

Encircled now
With all His crowns of glory:
Beneath His love reposing,
The whole redeem'd creation
  Is now at rest,
  For ever blest,
And sings His great salvation.

5 Break forth, O earth, in praises!
Dwell on His wondrous story;
  The Saviour's name
  And love proclaim—
The King who reigns in glory;
See on the throne beside Him,
O'er all her foes victorious,
  His royal bride,
  For whom He died,
Like Him for ever glorious.

CCXCIII.

"Blessed and holy is he that hath part in the First Resurrection."—Rev. xx. 6.

1 My life's a shade, my days
  Apace to death decline,—

My Lord is life, he'll raise
My flesh again, even mine.
Sweet truth to me,
I shall arise,
And with these eyes,
My Saviour see.

2 My peaceful grave shall keep
My bones till that sweet day
I wake from my long sleep,
And leave my bed of clay.
Sweet truth to me, &c.

3 My Lord His angels shall
Their golden trumpets sound,
At whose most welcome call
My grave shall be unbound.
Sweet truth to me, &c.

4 What means my beating heart,
To be afraid of death?
My life and I shan't part,
Tho' I resign my breath.
Sweet truth to me, &c.

5 I said sometimes with tears,
Ah, me! I'm loath to die;

Lord, silence thou these fears,
My life's with Thee on high.
Sweet truth to me, &c.

6 Then welcome, harmless grave,
By thee to Heaven I'll go;
My Lord His death shall save
Me from the flames below.
Sweet truth to me, &c.

CCXCIV.
"Behold the tabernacle of God is with men."—
Rev. xxi. 3.

1 HARK! the song of Jubilee,
Loud as mighty thunders roar,
Or the fulness of the sea
When it breaks upon the shore.
Hallelujah! for the Lord
God Omnipotent shall reign;
Hallelujah! let the word
Echo round the earth and main.

2 Hallelujah! hark, the sound
From the centre to the skies,
Wakes above, beneath, around,
All creation's harmonies.

See! Jehovah's banners furled,
  Sheath'd His sword—He speaks, 'tis done,
And the kingdoms of this world
  Are the kingdom of His Son.

3 He shall reign from pole to pole,
    With illimitable sway;
  He shall reign, when, like a scroll,
    Yonder Heavens have passed away:
  Then, the end;—beneath His rod
    Man's last enemy shall fall.
  Hallelujah! Christ in God,
    God in Christ is all in all.

CCXCV.

"He said unto me, it is done! I will give unto him that is athirst of the fountain of the water of life freely."—Rev. xxi. 6.

1 Time's sun is fast setting,
    Its twilight is nigh,
  Its evening is falling
    In cloud o'er the sky;
  Its shadows are stretching
    In ominous gloom;

Its midnight approaches—
The midnight of doom:
Then haste, sinner, haste, there is mercy for thee,
And wrath is preparing—flee, lingerer, flee!

2 Rides forth the fierce tempest
On the wing of the cloud;
The moan of the night-blast
Is fitful and loud;
The mountains are heaving,
The forests are bow'd,
The ocean is surging,
Earth gathers its shroud:
Then haste, sinner, haste, there is mercy for thee,
And wrath is preparing—flee, lingerer, flee!

3 The vision is nearing—
The Judge and the throne!—
The voice of the Angel
Proclaims " it is done."
On the whirl of the tempest
Its Ruler shall come,
And the blaze of His glory
Flash out from its gloom;
Then haste, sinner, haste, there is mercy for thee,
And wrath is preparing—flee, lingerer, flee!

4 With clouds He is coming!
   His people shall sing;
With gladness they hail Him
   Redeemer and King.
The iron rod wielding,
   The rod of His ire,
He cometh to kindle
   Earth's last fatal fire!
Then haste, sinner, haste, there is mercy for thee,
And wrath is preparing—flee, lingerer, flee!

CCXCVI.

"The city had no need of the sun."—Rev. xxi. 23.

1 There is a land of pure delight,
   Where saints immortal reign;
Infinite day excludes the night,
   And pleasures banish pain.

2 There everlasting spring abides,
   And never-withering flowers:
Death, like a narrow sea, divides
   This Heavenly land from ours.

3 Sweet fields beyond the swelling flood
   Stand dress'd in living green;

So to the Jews old Canaan stood,
    While Jordan roll'd between.

4 But timorous mortals start and shrink
    To cross this narrow sea,
  And linger, shivering on the brink,
    And fear to launch away.

5 O, could we but our doubts remove,
    These gloomy doubts that rise,
  And see the Canaan that we love,
    With unbeclouded eyes!

6 Could we but climb where Moses stood,
    And view the landscape o'er,
  Not Jordan's stream, nor death's cold flood,
    Should fright us from the shore.

CCXCVII.

"The Lamb is the light thereof."—Rev. xxi. 23.

1 THAT clime is not like this dull clime of ours;
    All, all is brightness there;
  A sweeter influence breathes around its flowers,
    And a far milder air.

No calm below is like that calm above,
No region here is like that realm of love;
Earth's softest spring ne'er shed so soft a light,
Earth's brightest summer never shone so bright.

2 That sky is not like this sad sky of ours,
    Tinged with earth's change and care:
No shadow dims it, and no rain-cloud lowers—
    No broken sunshine there!
One everlasting stretch of azure pours
Its stainless splendour o'er those sinless shores;
For there Jehovah shines with Heavenly ray,
There Jesus reigns dispensing endless day.

3 These dwellers there are not like those of earth,
    No mortal stain they bear;
And yet they seem of kindred blood and birth,—
    Whence and how came they there?
Earth was their native soil; from sin and shame,
Through tribulation they to glory came;
Bond slaves delivered from sin's crushing load,
Brands plucked from burning by the hand of God.

4 These robes of theirs are not like those below;
    No angel's half so bright!

Whence came that beauty, whence that living glow,
Whence came that radiant white?
Washed in the blood of the atoning Lamb,
Fair as the light these robes of theirs became,
And now, all tears wiped off from every eye,
They wander where the freshest pastures lie,
Through all the nightless day of that unfading sky.

CCXCVIII.

"He showed me a pure river of water of Life, clear as crystal, proceeding out of the throne of God and of the Lamb."—Rev. xxii. 1.

1 THERE is a stream, which issues forth
From God's eternal throne,
And from the Lamb, a living stream,
Clear as the crystal stone,
This stream doth water Paradise,
It makes the angels sing:
One cordial drop revives my heart,
Hence all my joys do spring.

2 Such joys as are unspeakable,
And full of glory too:
Such hidden manna, hidden pearls,
As worldlings do not know:

Eye hath not seen, nor ear hath heard,
　From fancy, tis conceal'd,
What Thou, Lord, hast laid up for thine,
　And hast to me reveal'd.

3 I see Thy face, I hear thy voice,
　I taste Thy richest love;
My soul doth leap; but, O for wings,
　The wings of Noah's dove:
Then would I flee far hence away,
　Leaving this world of sin;
Then would my Lord put forth His hand,
　And kindly take me in.

CCXCIX.

"They shall see His face; and His name shall be in their foreheads."—Rev. xxii. 4.

1 　What a rapturous song,
　　When the glorified throng,
　In the spirit of harmony join!
　　Join all the glad choirs,
　　Hearts, voices, and lyres,
　And the burden is mercy divine.

2 Hallelujah! they cry,
   To the King of the sky,
   To the great everlasting I AM!
   To the Lamb that was slain,
   And liveth again—
   Hallelujah to God and the Lamb!

3 The Lamb on the throne,
   Lo, He dwells with His own,
   And to rivers of pleasure He leads—
   With His mercy's full blaze,
   With the sight of His face,
   Our beatified spirits He feeds.

4 Our foreheads proclaim
   His ineffable name,
   Our bodies His glory display;
   A day without night,
   We feast in His sight,
   And eternity seems as a day!

CCC.

"Surely I come quickly."—Rev. xxii. 20.

1 Hope of our hearts! O Lord, appear,
   Thou glorious Star of day!

Shine forth and chase the dreary night,
With all our tears, away.

2 Strangers on earth, we wait for Thee:
O, leave the Father's throne;
Come with a shout of victory, Lord,
And claim us as Thine own.

3 O, bid the bright archangel then
The trump of God prepare,
To call Thy saints, the quick, the dead,
To meet Thee in the air.

4 No resting-place we seek on earth,
No loveliness we see;
Our eye is on the royal crown
Prepared for us and Thee.

5 But O, the thought of sharing, Lord,
Thy glorious throne above,
What is it to the brighter hope
Of dwelling in Thy love?

6 There, near Thy heart, upon Thy throne,
Thy ransom'd Bride shall see

What grace was in the bleeding Lamb
Who died to make her free.

CCCI.

"Even so, come, Lord Jesus."—Rev. xxii. 20.

The Church has waited long
  Her absent Lord to see;
And still in loneliness she waits,
  A friendless stranger she.
Age after age has gone,
  Sun after sun has set,
And still, in weeds of widowhood,
  She weeps a mourner yet.
    Come then, Lord Jesus, come!

2 Saint after saint on earth
  Has lived, and loved, and died,
And as they left us one by one,
  We laid them side by side;
We laid them down to sleep!
  But not in hope forlorn—
We laid them but to ripen there
  Till the last glorious morn.
    Come then, Lord Jesus, come!

3 The serpent's brood increase,
   The powers of hell grow bold,
The conflict thickens, faith is low
   And love is waxing cold.
How long, O Lord our God,
   Holy, and true, and good,
Wilt Thou not judge Thy suffering Church,
   Her sighs, and tears, and blood?
      Come, then, Lord Jesus, come!

4 We long to hear Thy voice,
   To see Thee face to face,
To share Thy crown and glory then.
   As now we share Thy grace.
Should not the loving Bride
   The absent Bridegroom mourn,
Should she not wear the weeds of grief
   Until her Lord return?
      Come, then, Lord Jesus, come!

5 The whole creation groans,
   And waits to hear that voice
That shall restore her comeliness,
   And make her wastes rejoice.

Come, Lord, and wipe away
The curse, the sin, the stain,
And make this blighted world of ours
Thine own fair world again.
Come then, Lord Jesus, come!

THE END.

WORKS BY THE REV. HORATIUS BONAR.

I.
THE NIGHT OF WEEPING.
18mo. 30 cents.

II.
THE MORNING OF JOY.
A SEQUEL TO THE ABOVE.
18mo. 40 cents.

III.
TRUTH AND ERROR.
18mo. 40 cents.

IV.
THE STORY OF GRACE.
18mo. 30 cents.

V.
MAN—HIS RELIGION AND HIS WORLD.
18mo. 40 cents.

VI.
A STRANGER HERE.
THE MEMORIAL OF ONE TO WHOM TO LIVE WAS CHRIST, AND TO DIE GAIN.
16mo. 75 cents.

VII.
THE BIBLE HYMN BOOK.
18mo. 50 cents.

BOOKS

PUBLISHED BY

Robert Carter & Brothers,

285 BROADWAY,

NEW YORK.

ABERCROMBIE'S Contest and the Armor. 32mo, gilt........ 25
ADAMS' Three Divine Sisters—Faith, Hope and Charity...... 50
ADVICE to a Young Christian. 18mo...................... 30
ALLEINE'S Gospel Promises. 18mo....................... 30
ALEXANDER'S Counsels to the Young. 32mo, gilt.......... 25
ANCIENT History of the Egyptians, Assyrians, &c. 2 vols.... 2 00
ANDERSON'S Annals of the English Bible. 8vo............. 1 75
——— Family Book. 12mo................................. 75
ANLEY'S Earlswood. A Tale............................. 75
ASHTON Cottage; or, The True Faith. Illustrated.......... 60
AUSTRALIA—The Loss of the Brig by Fire. 18mo.......... 25
BAGSTER—The Authenticity and Inspiration of the Bible.... 60
BALLANTYNE'S Mabel Grant. A Highland Story.......... 50
BAXTER'S Saint's Rest. Unabridged. 8vo................. 2 00
——— Call to the Unconverted. 18mo..................... 30
BIBLE Companion. Edited by Dr. Tyng................... 40
BIBLE Expositor. Illustrated. 18mo...................... 50
BICKERSTETH'S Treatise on Prayer. 18mo............... 40
——— Treatise on the Lord's Supper. 18mo................ 30
——— (E. H.) Waters from the Well Spring. 16mo.......... 60
BLOSSOMS of Childhood. 18mo.......................... 50
BLUNT'S Coincidences, and Paley's Horæ Paulinæ. 8vo..... 2 00
BOGATSKY'S Golden Treasury. 24mo, gilt................ 50
BOLTON'S Call to the Lambs. Illustrated................. 50
——— Tender Grass for Little Lambs...................... 50
BONAR'S (Rev. Horatius) Night of Weeping............... 30
——— Morning of Joy. A Sequel to the above............. 40
——— Story of Grace.................................... 30
——— Truth and Error. 18mo............................ 40
——— Man, his Religion and his World.................... 40
——— Eternal Day....................................... 50

BONAR'S (Rev. Andrew) Commentary on Leviticus. 8vo... 1 50
BONNET'S Family of Bethany. 18mo...................... 40
—— Meditations on the Lord's Prayer. 18mo............... 40
BOOTH'S Reign of Grace. 12mo......................... 75
BORROW'S Bible and Gypsies of Spain. 8vo, cloth.......... 1 00
BOSTON'S (Thomas) Select Works. Royal 8vo.............. 2 00
—— Four-fold State. 18mo............................. 50
—— Crook in the Lot. 18mo............................ 80
BRETT'S (Rev. W. H.) Indian Tribes of Guiana. 18mo....... 50
BREWSTER'S More Worlds than One..................... 60
BRIDGEMAN'S Daughter of China. 18mo................. 50
BRIDGES on the Christian Ministry. 8vo................. 1 50
—— on the Proverbs. 8vo............................. 2 00
—— on the CXIXth Psalm. 8vo......................... 1 00
—— Memoir of Mary J ne Graham. 8vo................. 1 00
BROKEN Bud; or, the Reminiscences of a Bereaved Mother. 75
BROTHER and Sister; or, the Way of Peace................ 50
BROWN'S (Rev. John, D.D.) Exposition of First Peter. 8vo.. 2 50
—— on the Sayings and Discourses of Christ. 2 vols. 8vo
—— on the Sufferings and Glories of the Messiah. 8vo..... 1 50
—— The Dead in Christ. 16mo......................... 50
BROWN'S Explication of the Assembly's Catechism. 12mo.. 60
BROWN (Rev. David) on the Second Advent. 12mo........ 1 25
BROWN'S Concordance. 32mo, gilt, 30 cents. Plain........ 20
BUCHANAN'S Comfort in Affliction. 18mo............... 40
—— on the Holy Spirit. 18mo.......................... 50
BUNBURY'S Glory, Glory, Glory, and other Narratives...... 25
BUNYAN'S Pilgrim's Progress. Fine ed. Large type. 12mo. 1 00
—— 18mo. Close type................................ 50
—— Jerusalem Sinner Saved. 18mo..................... 50
—— Greatness of the Soul. 18mo....................... 50
BURNS (John) Christian Fragments. 18mo................ 40
BUTLER'S (Bishop) Complete Works. 8vo................ 1 50
—— Sermons, alone. 8vo.............................. 1 00
—— Analogy, alone. 8vo.............................. 75
—— and Wilson's Analogy. 8vo........................ 1 25
CALVIN, The Life and Times of John Calvin. By Henry.... 2 00
CAMERON'S (Mrs.) Farmer's Daughter. Illustrated......... 80
CATECHISMS—The Assembly's Catechism. Per hundred.... 1 25
—— Do, with proofs............................ " " 3 00
—— Brown's Short Catechism......... ...... " " 1 25
—— Brown on the Assembly's Catechism. Each............ 10
—— Willison's Communicant's Catechism. Per dozen....... 75
CECIL'S Works. 3 vols. 12mo, with portrait............... 3 00
—— Sermons, separate ,,,,,,,,,,,,,,,,,,,,,,,,,,,,,,,,,, 1 00

CECIL'S Miscellanies and Remains, separate................. 1 00
—— Original Thoughts, separate........................ 1 00
—— (Catharine) Memoir of Mrs. Hawkes, with portrait...... 1 00
CHALMERS' Sermons. 2 vols. 8vo, with fine portrait....... 3 00
—— Lectures on Romans   "   "   " 1 50
—— Miscellanies   "   "   " 1 50
—— Select Works; comprising the above. 4 vols. 8vo..... 6 00
—— Evidences of Christian Revelation. 2 vols. 12mo...... 1 25
—— Natural Theology. 2 vols. 12mo..................... 1 25
—— Moral Philosophy.................................. 60
—— Commercial Discourses............................. 60
—— Astronomical Discourses........................... 60
CHARLES ROUSSEL; or, Honesty and Industry............. 40
CHARNOCK on the Attributes. 2 vols. 8vo............... 3 00
—— Choice Works...................................... 50
CHEEVER'S Lectures on the Pilgrim's Progress. Illus. 12mo. 1 00
—— Powers of the World to Come. 12mo................. 1 00
—— Right of the Bible in our Common Schools............ 75
CHILDS' Own Story Book. Square........................ 50
CHRISTIAN Retirement. 12mo............................ 75
—— Experience. By the same author. 12mo.............. 75
CLARA STANLEY; or, A Summer Among the Hills......... 50
CLAREMONT Tales (The). Illustrated. 18mo.............. 50
CLARK'S (Rev. John A.) Walk about Zion. 12mo......... 75
—— Pastor's Testimony................................. 75
—— Awake, Thou Sleeper.............................. 75
—— Young Disciple.................................... 88
—— Gathered Fragments............................... 1 00
CLARKE'S Daily Scripture Promises. 32mo, gilt........... 30
COLLIER'S Tale (The)................................... 25
COLQUHOUN'S (Lady) World's Religion. New edition. 16mo 50
COMMANDMENT, with Promise. 18mo.................... 40
COWPER'S Poetical Works. Complete. 2 vols. 16mo. Illus. 1 50
—— Task. Illustrated by Birket Foster.................. 4 50
CUMMING'S (Rev. John, D.D.) Message from God. 18mo.... 30
—— Christ Receiving Sinners. 18mo..................... 30
CUNNINGHAM'S World without Souls. 18mo.............. 30
CUYLER'S (Rev. T. L.) Stray Arrows. New edition......... 40
DAILY Commentary. For Family Reading. 8vo.......... 3 00
D'AUBIGNE'S History of the Reformation. 5 vols. 12mo.... 2 50
    Do.   do.   8vo. Complete in 1 vol.... 1 50
—— Life of Cromwell the Protector. 12mo................ 50
—— Germany, England and Scotland. 12mo.............. 75
—— Luther and Calvin. 18mo........................... 25
—— Authority of God. 16mo............................ 75

4   CARTERS' PUBLICATIONS.

DAVIDSON'S Connection of Sacred and Profane History 1 00
DAVID'S Psalms, in meter. Large type. 12mo. Embossed .. 75
   Do.   do.   do.   gilt edges 1 00
   Do.   do.   do.   Turkey morocco..... 2 00
   Do.   18mo. Good type. Plain sheep 83
   Do.   48mo. Very neat pocket edition. Sheep 20
   Do.   "   "   "   morocco.... 25
   Do.   "   "   "   gilt edges.. 81
   Do.   "   "   "   tucks 50
   Do.   with Brown's Notes. 18mo 50
   Do.   "   "   "   morocco, gilt 1 25
DAVIES' Sermons. 3 vols. 12mo 2 00
DICK'S (John, D.D.) Lectures on Theology. 2 vols. in 1. Cloth 2 50
   Do.   do.   do.   Sheep, $3. 2 vols. Cloth... 3 00
—— Lectures on Acts. 8vo 1 50
DICKINSON'S (Rev. R. W.) Scenes from Sacred History 1 00
—— Responses from Sacred Oracles 1 00
DILL'S Ireland's Miseries, their Cause and Cure 75
DODDRIDGE'S Rise and Progress. 18mo 40
—— Life of Colonel Gardiner. 18mo 80
DRUMMOND'S (Mrs.) Emily Vernon. A Tale. 16mo 75
—— (Rev. D. T. K.) on the Parables. 8vo ....
DUNCAN'S (Rev. Dr.) Sacred Philosophy of the Seasons. 2 vols. 2 50
—— Life, by his Son. With portrait. 12mo 75
—— Tales of the Scottish Peasantry. 18mo. Illustrated 50
—— Cottage Fireside. 18mo. Illustrated 40
—— (Mrs.) Life of Mary Lundie Duncan. 16mo 75
—— —— Life of George A. Lundie. 18mo 50
—— —— Memoir of George B. Phillips. 18mo 25
—— —— Children of the Manse 50
—— —— America as I Found It 1 00
—— (Mary Lundie) Rhymes for my Children. Illustrated.... 25
EDWARD'S (Jonathan, D.D.) Charity and its Fruits. 18mo... 50
ENGLISH Pulpit (The). 8vo 1 50
ERSKINE'S Gospel Sonnets. 18mo. Portrait 50
EVENING Hours with my Children. Colored, $1 75. Plain.. 1 25
EVIDENCES of Christianity—University of Virginia. 8vo.... 2 50
FAMILY Worship. 8vo. Morocco, $5. Half calf, $4. Cloth 3 00
FANNY and her Mamma. Square 50
FISK'S Memorial of the Holy Land, with steel plates 1 00
—— Orphan Tale 25
FLEETWOOD'S History of the Bible. Illustrated 2 00
FLORENCE Egerton; or, Sunshine and Shadow. Illustrated. 75
FOLLOW Jesus. By the author of " Come to Jesus" 25
FORD'S Decapolis. 18mo 25

CARTERS' PUBLICATIONS. 5

FOSTER'S Essays on Decision of Character, &c. 12mo........., 75
FOSTER'S Essays on the Evils of Popular Ignorance. 12mo.., 75
FOX'S Acts and Monuments. Complete. Illustrated........, 4 00
FRANK Harrison... 30
FRANK Netherton; or, the Talisman. 18mo................... 40
FRITZ Harold; or, the Temptation. 16mo.................... 60
FRY (Caroline) The Listener. Illustrated edition. 16mo...... 1 00
—— Christ our Law. 16mo................................... 60
—— Christ our Example and Autobiography. 16mo......... 75
—— Sabbath Musings. 18mo................................. 40
—— Scripture Reader's Guide. 18mo........................ 30
GELDART'S May Dundas. A Tale. 18mo.................... 50
GILFILLAN'S Martyrs, Heroes and Bards of Covenant. 16mo, 60
GOODE'S Better Covenant.................................... 60
GOODRICH'S Geography of the Bible.........................
GRAY'S Poems. Illust. Mor. $2 50. Gilt extra $1 50. Plain 1 00
HALDANE'S (Robert) Exposition of Romans. 8vo............ 2 50
—— (Robert and James A.) Lives. 8vo...................... 2 00
HAMILTON'S (Rev. James, D.D.) Life in Earnest. 18mo...... 30
—— Mount of Olives. 18mo................................. 30
—— Harp on Willows. 18mo................................ 30
—— Thankfulness, and other Essays. 18mo................. 30
—— Life of Hall. 32mo, gilt................................ 30
—— Lamp and Lantern. 18mo.............................. 40
—— Happy Home. 18mo.................................... 50
—— Life of Lady Colquhoun. 16mo......................... 75
—— Life of Richard Williams. 16mo........................ 75
—— Royal Preacher. 16mo................................. 85
HAWKER'S Poor Man's Morning Portion. 12mo............. 60
Do   do.   Evening Portion. 12mo............. 60
—— Zion's Pilgrim. 18mo.... 30
HENRY'S Commentary. 5 vols. Quarto. Fine edition......
—— Miscellaneous Works. 2 vols. Royal 8vo.............. 4 00
—— Method for Prayer. . 18mo............................. 40
—— Communicant's Companion. 18mo..................... 40
—— Daily Communion with God. 18mo.................... 30
—— Pleasantness of a Religious Life. 24mo, gilt........... 30
HENRY (Philip) Life of. 18mo..... 50
HERVEY'S Meditations. 18mo.............................. 40
HETHERINGTON'S History of the Church of Scotland. 8vo.. 1 50
—— History of Westminster Assembly. 12mo............. 75
—— Minister's Family. A Tale............................ 75
HEWITSON, Memoir of the Rev. W. H. Hewitson. 12mo.... 85
HILL'S (George) Lectures on Divinity. 8vo................ 2 00
HISTORIC Doubts... 50

HISTORY of the Puritans and Pilgrim Fathers. 12mo........ 1 00
HISTORY of the Reformation in Europe. 18mo.............. 40
HOOKER (Rev. H.), The Uses of Adversity. 18mo........... 30
——— Philosophy of Unbelief. 12mo....................... 75
HORNE'S Introduction. 2 vols. Royal 8vo. Half cloth...... 3 50
    Do.   1 vol., sheep, $4. 2 vols., sheep, $5. 2 vols., cloth. 4 00
HORNE'S (Bishop) Commentary on the Book of Psalms. 8vo. 1 50
HOWARD (John); or, the Prison World of Europe. 16mo.... 75
HOWELL'S Life—Perfect Peace. 18mo...................... 30
HOWE'S Redeemer's Tears. 18mo.......................... 50
HOWIE'S Scots Worthies. 8vo............................. 1 50
HUSS (John) Life of. Translated from the German......... 25
INFANT'S Progress. 18mo. Illustrated.................... 50
JACOBUS on Matthew. With a Harmony. Illustrated....... 75
——— on Mark and Luke................................. 75
——— on John and Acts (preparing)..................... 75
——— Catechetical Questions on each vol. Per dozen..... 1 50
JAMES' Anxious Inquirer. 18mo........................... 30
——— Christian Progress. 18mo.......................... 30
——— True Christian. 18mo.............................. 30
——— Widow Directed. 18mo............................. 30
——— Young Man from Home. 18mo...................... 30
——— Christian Professor. 16mo......................... 75
——— Christian Duty. 16mo............................. 75
——— Christian Father's Present. 16mo................. 75
——— Course of Faith. 16mo............................ 75
——— Young Woman's Friend. 16mo..................... 75
——— Young Man's Friend. 16mo........................ 75
JAMIE Gordon; or, the Orphan. Illustrated. 18mo.......... 50
JANEWAY'S Heaven upon Earth. 18mo.................... 50
——— Token for Children. 18mo.......................... 50
JAY'S Morning and Evening Exercises. Large type. 4 vols.. 4 00
    Do.   do.   Cheap edition. 2 vols........ 1 50
——— Autobiography and Reminiscences. 2 vols. 12mo..... 2 50
——— Female Scripture Characters. 12mo................. 1 00
——— Christian Contemplated. 18mo...................... 40
JEANIE Morrison; or, the Discipline of Life. 16mo.......... 75
    By the same Author.
    A New Volume, uniform with the above............... 75
    THE Pastor's Family. 18mo........................... 25
JOHNSON'S Rasselas. Elegant edition. 16mo............... 50
KENNEDY'S (Grace) Profession is not Principle. 18mo...... 30
——— Father Clement. 18mo............................. 30
——— Anna Ross. 18mo. Illustrated..................... 30
——— Philip Colville. A Covenanter's Story............... 30

KENNEDY'S Decision. 18mo.................................. 25
——— Jessy Allan, the Lame Girl. 18mo..................... 25
KEY to the Shorter Catechism. 18mo........................ 20
KING'S (Rev. David, L.L.D.) Geology and Religion. 16mo.... 75
——— on the Eldership.................................... 50
KITTO'S Daily Bible Illustrations. 8 vols. 12mo........... 8 00
——— Lost Senses... 1 00
KRUMMACHER'S Martyr Lamb. 18mo............................ 40
——— Elijah the Tishbite. 18mo........................... 40
——— Last Days of Elisha. 18mo........................... 50
LAW and Testimony. By Miss Warner. 8vo.................... 3 00
LEYBURN'S Soldier of the Cross. 12mo...................... 1 00
LIFE in New York. 18mo.................................... 40
LIFE of a Vagrant. Written by himself. 18mo............... 30
LIGHTED Valley; or, the Memoir of Miss Bolton............. 75
LITTLE Annie's First Book. Square......................... 35
——— Annie's Second do. Square............................ 40
LITTLE Lessons for Little Learners. Square................ 50
LIVING to Christ.. 40
LUTHER'S Commentary on the Galatians. 8vo................. 1 50
MACKAY, The Wycliffites................................... 75
——— Family at Heatherdale. 18mo......................... 50
MAMMA'S Bible Stories..................................... 50
  Do.   do.   Sequel................................... 50
MARSHALL on Sanctification. 18mo.......................... 50
MARTYRS and Covenanters of Scotland. 18mo................. 40
McCHEYNE'S (Rev. Robert Murray) Works. 2 vols. 8vo........ 3 00
——— Life, Lectures and Letters. Separate................ 1 50
——— Sermons. Separate................................... 2 00
McCLELLAND (Prof. Alex.) on the Canon and Interpretation.. 75
McCOSH on the Divine Government, Physical and Moral....... 2 00
McCRINDELL, The Convent. A Narrative. 18mo................ 50
——— The School Girl in France. 16mo.................... 50
McFARLANE, The Mountains of the Bible. Illustrated........ 75
McGHEE'S (Rev. R. J.) Lectures on the Ephesians. 8vo...... 2 00
McILVAINE'S Truth and Life. A Series of Discourses........ 2 00
MEIKLE'S Solitude Sweetened. 12mo......................... 60
MENTEATH, Lays of the Kirk and Covenant. Illust. 16mo..... 75
MICHAEL Kemp, The Happy Farmer's Lad. 18mo................ 40
MILLER (Hugh), The Geology of the Bass Rock. Illustrated.. 75
MISSIONARY of Kilmany..................................... 40
MISSIONS, The Origin and History of. 25 steel plates. 4to.. 8 50
MOFFAT'S Southern Africa. 12mo............................ 75
MONOD'S Lucilla; or, the Reading of the Bible. 18mo....... 40
MOORE (Rev. T. V.) Com. on Haggai, Zechariah and Malachi.

MORE'S (Hannah) Private Devotion. 18mo.................... 30
Do.   do.   do.   32mo. 20 cents. Gilt... 30
MORELL'S History of Modern Philosophy. 8vo.............. 3 00
MORNING of Life. 18mo................................... 40
MORNING and Night Watches.............................. 60

By the same Author:—
    FOOTSTEPS of St. Paul. 12mo. Illustrated........... 1 00
    FAMILY Prayers. 12mo............................... 75
    WOOD-CUTTER of Lebanon, and Exiles of Lucerna.... 50
    THE Great Journey. Illustrated..................... 50
    THE Words of Jesus................................. 40
    THE Mind of Jesus.................................. 40
MY School-Boy Days. 18mo. Illustrated................. 80
MY Youthful Companions. 18mo Illustrated.............. 80
    The above two in one volume....................... 50
NEW Cobwebs to Catch Little Flies...................... 50
NEWTON'S (Rev. John) Works. 2 vols. in 1. Portrait..... 2 00
NOEL'S Infant Piety. 18mo.............................. 25
OBERLIN (John Frederick) Memoirs of.................... 40
OLD White Meeting-House. 18mo.......................... 40
OLD Humphrey's Observations — Addresses — Thoughts for
    Thoughtful—Walks in London—Homely Hints—Country
    Strolls—Old Sea Captain—Grand parents—Isle of Wight—
    Pithy Papers—Pleasant Tales—North American Indians,
    12 vols. 18mo. Each................................ 40
OPIE on Lying. New edition. 18mo. Illustrated.......... 40
OSBORNE (Mrs.) The World of Waters. Illustrated. 18mo... 50
OWEN on Spiritual Mindedness. 12mo.................... 60
PALEY'S Evidences. Edited by Prof. Nairne.............. 1 25
    —— Horæ Paulinæ. 8vo............................. 75
PASCAL (Jaqueline); or, Convent Life in Port Royal. 12mo.. 1 00
    —— Provincial Letters............................. 1 00
PASTOR'S Daughter. By Louisa Payson Hopkins........... 40
PATTERSON on the Assembly's Shorter Catechism......... 50
PEARSON on Infidelity. Fine edition. 8vo. $2. Cheap ed... 60
PEEP of Day.. 30

By the same Author:—
    LINE upon Line.................................... 30
    PRECEPT on Precept................................ 30
    NEAR Home... 50
    FAR Off... 50
    SCRIPTURE Facts................................... 50
PHILIP'S Devotional Guides. 2 vols..................... 1 50
—— Young Man's Closet Library......................... 75

PHILIP'S Mary's, Martha's, Lydia's and Hannah's Love of the
    Spirit. Each... 40
PIKE'S True Happiness. 18mo............................. 30
—— Divine Origin of Christianity.................. 30
POLLOK'S Course of Time. Elegant edition. 16mo. Portrait 1 00
—— Do. 18mo. Small copy. Close type............. 40
—— Life, Letters and Remains. By the Rev. J. Scott, D.D... 1 00
—— Tales of the Scottish Covenanters. Illustrated.......... 50
—— Helen of the Glen. 18mo. Illustrated................. 25
—— Persecuted Family   "   "   25
—— Ralph Gemmell   "   "   25
POOL'S Annotations. 3 vols. 8vo. Half calf, $12. Cloth.... 10 00
PRAYERS of St. Paul. 16mo.............................. 75
QUARLE'S Emblems. Illustrated.......................... 1 00
RETROSPECT (The). By Aliquis. 18mo.................... 40
RICHMOND'S Domestic Portraiture. Illustrated. 16mo...... 75
—— Annals of the Poor. 18mo............................ 40
RIDGELY'S Body of Divinity. 2 vols. Royal 8vo............ 4 00
ROGER Miller; or, Heroism in Humble Life. 18mo.......... 30
ROGER'S Jacob's Well. 18mo............................. 40
—— Folded Lamb. 18mo................................ 40
ROMAINE on Faith. 12mo................................ 60
—— Letters. 12mo..................................... 60
RUTHERFORD'S Letters. With Life by Bonar.............. 1 50
RYLE'S Living or Dead. A Series of Home Truths.......... 75
—— Wheat or Chaff.................................... 75
—— Startling Questions................................ 75
—— Rich and Poor.................................... 75
—— Priest, Puritan and Preacher........................ 75
SAPHIR (Philip) Life of.................................. 30
SCHMID'S Hundred Short Tales........................... 50
SCOTIA'S Bards. A Collection of the Scottish Poets.......... 2 00
SCOTT'S Daniel. A Model for Young Men.................. 1 50
—— (Thos.) Force of Truth. 18mo....................... 25
SELECT Works of James Venn, Wilson, Philip and Jay...... 1 50
—— Christian Authors. 2 vols. 8vo..................... 2 00
SELF Explanatory Bible. Half calf, $4 50. Morocco........ 6 00
SERLE'S Christian Remembrancer......................... 50
SHERWOOD'S Clever Stories. Square..................... 50
—— Jack the Sailor Boy................................ 25
—— Duty is Safety.................................... 25
—— Think before you Act.............................. 25
SINNER'S Friend. 18mo................................. 25
SIGOURNEY'S (Mrs. L. H.) Water Drops. Illust. 16mo...... 75
—— Letters to my Pupils. With portrait. 16mo.......... . 75

SIGOURNEY'S Memoir of Mrs. L. H. Cook	75
—— Olive Leaves	50
—— Faded Hope	50
—— Boy's Book. 18mo	40
—— Girl's Book. 18mo	40
—— Child's Book. Square	35
SINCLAIR'S Modern Accomplishments	75
—— Modern Society	75
—— Hill and Valley	75
—— Holyday House	50
—— Charlie Seymour	30
SMITH'S (Rev. James) Green Pastures for the Lord's Flock	1 00
SMYTH'S Bereaved Parents Consoled. 12mo	75
SONGS in the House of my Pilgrimage. 16mo	75
SORROWING yet Rejoicing	30
STEVENSON'S Christ on the Cross. 12mo	75
—— Lord our Shepherd. 12mo	60
—— Gratitude. 12mo	75
STORIES on the Lord's Prayer	30
STUCKLEY'S Gospel Glass	75
SUMNER'S Exposition of Matthew and Mark. 12mo	75
SYMINGTON on Atonement. 12mo	75
TALES from English History. Illustrated	75
TAYLOR'S (Jane) Hymns for Infant Minds. Square. Illust	40
—— Rhymes for the Nursery. Square. Illustrated	50
—— Limed Twigs to Catch Young Birds. Square. Illust	50
—— Life and Correspondence. 18mo	40
—— Display. A Tale. 18mo	30
—— Original Poems and Poetical Remains. Illustrated	40
—— (Isaac) Loyola; or, Jesuitism in its Rudiments	1 00
—— —— Natural History of Enthusiasm	75
—— (Jeremy) Sermons. Complete in 1 vol. 8vo	1 50
TENNENT'S Life	25
THEOLOGICAL Sketch Book. 2 vols	3 00
THREE Months under the Snow. 18mo	30
THORNWELL'S Discourses on Truth	1 00
TUCKER, The Rainbow in the North. 18mo	50
—— Abbeokuta or, Sunrise in the Tropics. 18mo	50
—— The Southern Cross and the Southern Crown	75
TURNBULLS Genius of Scotland. Illustrated. 16mo	1 00
—— Pulpit Orators of France and Switzerland	1 00
TYNG'S Lectures on the Law and Gospel. With portrait	1 50
—— Christ is All. 8vo. With portrait	1 50
—— Israel of God. 8vo. Enlarged edition	1 50
—— Rich Kinsman	2 00

CARTERS' PUBLICATIONS. 11

TYNG'S Recollections of England. 12mo.	1 00
—— Christian Titles.	75
—— A Lamb from the Flock. 18mo.	25
VARA; or, the Child of Adoption.	1 00
VERY Little Tales, First and Second Series. 2 vols.	75
WARDLAW on Miracles.	75
WATERBURY'S Book of the Sabbath. 18mo.	40
WATSON'S Body of Divinity. 8vo.	2 00
WATTS' Divine Songs. Illustrated. Square.	40
WEEK (The). Illustrated. 16mo.	50
WHATELY'S Kingdom of Christ and Errors of Romanism.	75
WHITECROSS' Anecdotes on Assembly's Catechism.	80
WHITE'S (Hugh) Meditations on Prayer. 18mo.	40
—— Believer. A Series of Discourses. 18mo.	40
—— Practical Reflections on the Second Advent. 18mo.	40
—— (Henry Kirke) Complete Works. Life by Southey.	1 00
WILBERFORCE'S (Wm.) Practical View. Large type. 12mo.	1 00
—— Life. By Mary A. Collier.	75
WILLISON'S Sacramental Meditations and Advices. 18mo.	50
WILSON'S Lights and Shadows of Scottish Life. 16mo. Illust.	75
WINSLOW on Personal Declension and Revival.	60
—— Midnight Harmonies.	60
WOODROOFFE'S Shades of Character.	1 50
WYLIE'S Journey over the Region of Fulfilled Prophecy.	80
YOUNG'S Night Thoughts. 16mo. Large type, with portrait	1 00
Do " " Extra gilt, $1 50. Mor. $2. 18mo.	40

BOOKS NOT STEREOTYPED.

BICKERSTETH'S Works. 16 vols. 16mo.	10 00
—— On John and Jude.	60
BINNEY'S Make the Best of Both Worlds.	60
BRIDGES' Manual for the Young.	50
BUXTON (Sir T. F.), A Study for Young Men.	50
CHART of Sacred History. Folio.	1 50
DA COSTA'S Israel and the Gentiles. 12mo.	1 25
—— Four Witnesses.	2 00
EADIE on Colossians.	
—— on Ephesians.	8 00
FLETCHER'S Addresses to the Young.	60
HALL'S Forum and the Vatican.	1 00
HEWITSON'S Remains. 2 vols.	2 00

HOWELL'S Remains... 75
LONDON Lectures to Young Men, 1853-4................... 1 00
  "   "   "   1854-5................... 1 00
MALAN'S Pictures from Switzerland........................ 60
OWEN'S Works. 16 vols. 8vo............................. 20 00
PRATT (Josiah) Memoirs of................................ 1 50
SMITH'S (Jno. Pye) Scripture Testimony to Messiah.......... 5 00
SELF-EXPLANATORY Bible, half calf, $4,50 mor............ 6 00
SWETE'S Family Prayers................................. 60
THOLUCK'S Hours of Devotion............................ 60
VILLAGE Churchyard. 18mo.............................. 40
——— Pastor. 18mo.................................... 40
——— Observer. 18mo.................................. 30
WILSON (Prof.), The Forester, a Tale....................... 75
WORDS to Win Souls. 12mo............................... 75

THE FIRESIDE SERIES.

A Series of beautiful volumes of the Narrative kind, uniform in binding, and prettily Illustrated. 18mo. Price 50 cents each.

The following are now ready:

MABEL GRANT. A Highland Story.
THE WOODCUTTER OF LEBANON.
LOUIS AND FRANK.
CLARA STANLEY. A Story for Girls.
THE CLAREMONT TALES.
THE CONVENT. By Miss M'Crindell.
FAR OFF. By the author of the "Peep of Day."
NEAR HOME. By the same author.
HAPPY HOME. By Dr. Hamilton.
JAMIE GORDON; or, the Orphan.
THE CHILDREN OF THE MANSE. By Mrs. Duncan.
TALES OF THE SCOTTISH PEASANTRY.
SCHOOL DAYS AND COMPANIONS.
THE INDIAN TRIBES OF GUIANA.
HOLIDAY HOUSE. By Miss Sinclair.
OLIVE LEAVES. By Mrs. Sigourney.
BROTHER AND SISTER.
POLLOK'S TALES OF THE COVENANTERS.
THE RAINBOW IN THE NORTH.
THE INFANT'S PROGRESS. By Mrs. Sherwood.
THE WORLD OF WATERS.
BLOSSOMS OF CHILDHOOD.
MAY DUNDAS. A Tale.
ABBEOKUTA; or, Sunrise in the Tropics.
THE FAMILY AT HEATHERDALE.

www.ingramcontent.com/pod-product-compliance
Lightning Source LLC
Chambersburg PA
CBHW032014220426
43664CB00006B/242